THE VILLAGE OF MEINCIAU

THE VILLAGE
OF MEINCIAU

Mansel Thomas

Published by
MANSEL THOMAS

Published by
Mansel Thomas
Tŷ Gwyn, Mynyddygarreg
Kidwelly, Carmarthenshire, SA17 4RA

ISBN 978-0-9570831-0-3

Printed and bound in Wales by
Dinefwr Press Ltd.
Rawlings Road, Llandybie
Carmarthenshire, SA18 3YD

This book is dedicated to:

Eleri, Carys, Eurig and the grandchildren – strong roots
help to develop a sense of identity.

In memory of my parents, Jack and Eirwen Thomas
and to the people of Meinciau past and present.

All proceeds made from the sale of this book
will be donated to
Ail Gyfle/Second Chance Cancer Appeal.

Charity Number 1107239.

Contents

Introduction

Writing this book has given me enormous pleasure. I feel it is a privilege to have had the opportunity to write about my home village and its locality. After living in Porthcawl for a number of years we, as a family, moved back to the area and, by now, we have lived in Mynyddygarreg for over 35 years. There is always a danger when looking back to see the past through rose tinted spectacles but, hopefully, there are not many sins of commission but I am sure that there are many sins of omission. However, one day the baton may be picked up by someone else who will continue and expand on what is contained between these covers.

Braslun o Hanes Eglwys Moreia Meinciau 1827-1965 by W. J. Rhys was a sound base for the chapter on Moreia chapel.

The staff members of the Llanelli and Carmarthen Libraries and the Archives in Carmarthen were always accommodating and helpful.

Discussions with many local people, too numerous to mention, has been a source of valuable information. I am also thankful to the people who have given photographs for inclusion in the book.

I am greatly indebted to Elsbeth Jones for scrutinising the script and correcting the numerous mistakes.

I am grateful to Dianne, my wife, for her patience, support, advice and the endless cups of tea and coffee that made their way upstairs to my little hideaway.

I am extremely thankful to Llangyndeyrn Community Council for their very generous financial support and also to County Councillor Tyssul Evans for his generous contribution to this project.

A Diagram of Meinciau and District

(Not drawn to scale)

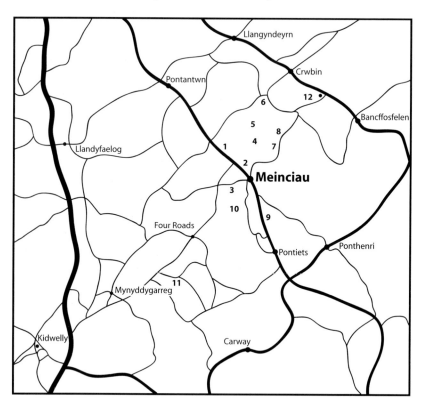

1. Blaenyfan Quarry
2. Fferm Blaen y Fan
3. Meinciau Mawr
4. Gellygatrog
5. Laswern
6. Capel Dyddgen
7. Torcefen
8. Gwndwn Mawr
9. Ysgol Gwynfryn
10. Gwndwn Bach
11. Parc Matho
12. Garn Ganol

The Meaning of Meinciau

According to the *Dictionary Of The Place Names Of Wales* there is a reference to the village in 1760 as Mancha, Min Key in 1765, Maingieu in 1831, y Meincau in 1839, Minkau in 1851 and, finally, Meinciau in 1920.

Mainc means bench and the plural of mainc is meinciau. When looking at the terrain from both Pontiets and Pontantwn up towards Meinciau a series of low hills and banks can be identified representing a series of "benches". This could be one possible meaning for the name.

It is also possible that the name derives from "min y cae" – edge of the field – which might be linked to the period of land enclosures.

Years ago Minkie was common on many signposts – this came about because many people who had come from England found it difficult to pronounce the word Meinciau, and conseqently Meinciau became Minkie. That, thank goodness, by now belongs to the past!

We as natives however always refer to the village as Minke (pronounced as Minke . . . e as in elephant)

The Whitewashed Cottages

In my opinion these wonderful and quaint cottages, characteristic of many houses found in Wales around the middle of the eighteenth century, gave the village an unique character. Situated right in the middle of the village it was these cottages that made the place what it was. They provided the visitor with an image of Meinciau and the picture that would be conjured up whenever the village was mentioned. Disastrously, they were demolished in the mid 1960s to make room for new and modern bungalows. I do not for one moment dispute the need for new housing but surely there was an alternative to what was actually done.

These ground floor cottages were either one or two roomed with the 'Tŷ Cornel' resembling a penthouse suite with its two front doors – one on the main road and the other on the *Hewl Dop*. In my time this was the home of Harding and Ross Jones. They also acquired the one room cottage which was next door on the Hewl Dop. Next door to this one room cottage was 'Tŷ Canol' with its two rooms and the end cottage was 'Tŷ Top' or 'Tŷ Uchaf', the home of the grand old lady of the village Mrs Lydia Evans and her granddaughter Mary. Opposite this cottage was the home of Willie and Sarah Walters. Next door to Tŷ Cornel on the main Llanelli–Carmarthen road was Plasbach better known as Siop Ley. Meinciau Mawr farm, Meinciau Bach, Blaenlline, Morning Star and Delfryn were all part of the same estate.

From what I understand all these houses, including the Black Horse together with other houses and farms in and around the village, were part of the Stepney Estate which belonged to the Stepney family based in Llanelli. But in 1827 the Stepney estate passed from the Stepney family to the Chambers family as a result of an unusual and complicated will. According to the 1846 records William Chambers was the landlord and eventually William Chambers Junior took over the reins. But after William Chambers Senior died in 1855 the Stepney family took steps to regain the estate and after lengthy litigation the estate returned to the Stepneys. Until his death in 1930 the landlord was Richard Wilson Phillips of the Vicarage,

The village square with the Black Horse on the right and Siop Ley on the immediate left, next door to Tŷ Cornel.

Pendine. In his will dated May 11th 1927 he noted that his niece, Henrietta Catherine Moore, of Coombe Down, Bath, was to inherit these properties on his death.

In 1954 Henrietta, who was a spinster, died and the properties were transferred to Edel Mary Moore of the same address. She was a spinster as well and she died two years later. However, there was another name on the deeds – that of John Eustace Rosser. Who this person was is a mystery but within another year the cottages became the property of Cuthbert James Garner Moore of the Shell Company in the city of Cape Town, South Africa, and Caroline Hartford also of Cape Town. For many years it was a person by the name of John Saer who collected the rent and many believed that it was him who actually owned the properties but he was only the agent to the actual landowners. By 1964 the Cape Town landowners only owned Tŷ Cornel with rest of the cottages having been bought in the preceding years by Wil Evans Brynbarre. Meinciau Mawr, Meinciau Bach and Blaenlline had all in the meantime been bought by the tenants. In 1964 all the whitewashed cottages including Plasbach were sold to Carmarthenshire County Council who in turn demolished them in order to build six new bungalows at what became known as Bryn Moreia.

There was a need for new housing but the act of demolishing the old cottages was a betrayal of the village's heritage. The bungalows could

13

have been built elsewhere in the village. A few years ago I travelled with my family from Oban to The Mull of Kintyre in Scotland. Along the journey we came across a row of cottages very similar to the cottages in Meinciau. Nobody lived in them any more but they now played their role in the tourist industry. I am afraid that we in Wales have a great deal to learn when it comes to attracting tourists and to preserve what is of importance from the past. There is a distinct lack of vision and foresight on the part of people that make these crucial decisions.

By today the village is much larger with the development of The Ashes, Maes Hywel, Heol Meinciau Mawr and along Heol y Meinciau towards Pontiets.

The Village Pump

The village pump was a natural meeting and communication point in the village. Before water was made available on tap in every house the water pump was an essential point of call for every householder every day and several times a day very often. It was a meeting point where the burning issues of the day were discussed and digested – these issues being of both national and of local importance. No doubt it was also the arena where various Chinese whispers would be conceived. The bus stop was also located by the village pump and this again underlined the importance of the location.

It was a meeting point for the youngsters especially after the Sunday night service. The old pump was witness to a great deal of hilarity and playfulness. Many a romance began around the old pump and it was a stage for some posturing in the quest for recognition from the opposite sex. It was also extremely convenient when the baptism services were held since the actual baptistery was the other side of the wall.

Eventually the importance of the village pump disappeared. Every house had its own water supply but the old pump remained as a symbol of a previous age. For some strange reason the County Council decided to move the old pump to Llyn Brianne and it was replaced with another. Unfortunately, however, this was stolen and although it was eventually replaced, that very act says a great deal about sections of today's society.

Childhood Memories

Home is home – the home where we now live, but it can also be the place where we were born and grew up. Some people have always lived in the same home since they were born. Torcefen was my home – a small forty acre farm just over half a mile from the village square on the road that leads from Meinciau to Bancffosfelen known as the Hewl Dop, or Hewl y Mynydd or even Hewl y Banc. It must be a very important road to have all those names!

My very first memories go back to 1947 and to the huge snowfall of that winter with people endeavouring to clear the snow that lay deep up to hedge height along the road. I remember, as a three-year-old, the fascination of walking on top of the snow drifts and even looking down on the hedges below.

I also remember travelling in the horse and cart with Non, my grand-father, on some mission to Pontantwn as well as the occasional visit to the blacksmith Gof y Cnoc in Mynyddygarreg. We travelled in a beautiful blue cart with huge red wooden wheels supporting a steel rim perimeter, pulled by "Blackes" which, as the name suggests, was a large black shire horse.

The horse was kept in the stable that doubled up as the sleeping quarters for John Bowen, a man of no fixed abode, who shared the same name as my grandfather. John Bowen y Stabal, as he was known locally, had lost his way and he shared his living quarters not only with "Blackes" but also with the occasional rat as well as the numerous mice that dwelled in such a splendid hotel. It is no wonder that my mother would not consider for one moment my requests to sleep with John in the stable!

I was on friendly terms with many of the animals and the annual killing of the pig, sometime in the autumn, was a day that I always dreaded. The night before the execution I would visit my friend in the condemned cell and explain to him that I had nothing to do with what was going to happen the following morning. I convinced myself that the pig understood my situation and we would say our goodbyes. There was no way that I could face my friend in the morning and I would find my way to the furthest field to escape the inevitable screeching that would precede the conclusion of life for yet another pig.

The slaughter of the pig was an important day. The pig would be tied, hauled and lifted on to a sturdy wooden bench. It would require at least three or four men to accomplish this feat and to hold the pig down while its throat was slit in the appropriate place. After the actual kill a plentiful supply of hot water was necessary to soften the hair, thus enabling an easier shave. The pig would be opened and hung up. The following day it would be cut into substantial pieces which, in turn, would be salted. This was a supply of meat that would last the whole winter and often well into the summer. It was traditional when jointing the meat to share some of it with the neighbours as well as the faggots which my mother made. One part of the pig was eaten on the very night it was cut up and that was the *"gwningen"* or the loin. While eating that particular delicious piece of meat my intimate conversation with the pig was conveniently forgotten! The slabs of salted meat would lie in the cold room (*llaethdy*) for weeks before it would eventually be hung from the high ceiling in the kitchen until needed. A long needle would occasionally be inserted into the meat during the following months to ensure that it was in good condition.

One of my first memories of the work carried out on the farm was the carting of the manure from the dung heap, *"domen dail."* The manure would be carried in a cart pulled by the horse and spread in regular heaps on the field. These heaps would later be dispersed with a fork and so the manure would be spread all over the field. This was hard work and far too difficult for a small boy to handle. In contrast, haymaking to me was a pleasurable sequence of tasks, something to look forward to although my contribution was minimal during those early days, I thoroughly enjoyed the haymaking season. It was a great social occasion, with neighbouring farmers helping each other. However, it was hard work for the grown ups. I remember the time when the hay was gathered in bundles on the field before being collected in the cart and taken to the rickyard (*yr ydlan*) to be stacked either in ricks or in the hayshed. This was the custom before the age of the tractor. After this metal horse became a normal part of farming life, the common haymaking picture was that of the tractor pulling the trailer attached to the hayloader which lifted the hay from its rows on to the trailer. Later on the baler came on the scene. It was essential to load the neatly packed rectangular bales carefully onto the trailer and there was a special way of stacking them. By today most farmers have contractors bringing in their huge and expensive machines in order to harvest the silage or the "big bales" be they round, square or oblong.

I may be romanticising but I believe that the excitement and the special aura of those haymaking days of my childhood have been irretrievably lost. In those days neighbours got together and found time to take a breather and shelter from the sweltering sun; they would drink tea, or even something stronger and guzzle their way through a mountain of sandwiches and *bara brith*. At the same time the buzz of local gossip would fill the air heavily drenched with the sweet and comforting smell of new mown hay. After a great deal of leg pulling and laughter, it was then back to work. In Torcefen it was customary to have a barrel of beer or cider to quench the considerable thirst of the haymakers. On one occasion a certain family member from the village came to help us. Quietly he kept giving me swigs of cider, which I readily accepted and, I suppose, enjoyed. I was only seven at the time and I remember very little of the afternoon! I spent the rest of the day in bed, completely oblivious of the fact that Ron Ynys Fach had turned up to play with me.

My mother, to put it mildly, was rather annoyed and I cannot remember my friend, who quenched my thirst that afternoon, ever having the chance to help out after that. As I grew up there was an ever increasing expectation for me to pull my weight and help. It was then that I realised that haymaking was not such a romantic, pleasurable social event after all but really hard work. By today of course the modern machinery does all the work and the stresses are different in nature.

To me Meinciau was the centre of the world. Sadly by today huge pylons dominate the skyline. We were told that they would only be there for twenty years. Almost fifty years later they still tower over the village. All such power lines should be underground. The village had no Woolworth, British Home Stores or Sainsburys but it did have its Siop Ley which will be discussed in another chapter. Siop Sâr was not only the village post office but the local takeaway as well – only that the takeaway would be eaten on the premises. The takeaway comprised of peaches, pears and apricots, being eaten straight from the tin together with slices of bread and butter prepared by Sara. Running this homely shop were Sara, William Davey and her unmarried sister Catherine. Sara was married to William Davey (or

Dai Pencwm) who was a number of years younger than his wife, although he was not a spring chick himself. He was as wide as he was tall. I vaguely remember him playing left back for Meinciau Rovers. Sara was the news service for the village; she was the fountain of all the local gossip. There was no need to buy the *Carmarthen Journal* Sara was the *Journal*!

Moreia Chapel was the focal point and the heart of the village. But the Black Horse was also a focal point and most of the local people who frequented the Black were also regular members of Moreia. However, it is fair to say that a few of the Moreia faithfuls did not frequent the Black – well not through the front door anyway! It is no wonder that Moreia is a Baptist chapel. As a child I believed that we, as villagers, knew God and that God knew us. To start with Meinciau was closer to Heaven than Pontiets and Four Roads and certainly closer than the unfortunate inhabitants of Mynyddygarreg. As for Kidwelly – it was on another planet!

In the early 1950s Sunday was still a sacred day, in its fullest meaning, in the lives of many families in the area. Only the absolutely essential work would be carried out on Sundays. Even preparing the Sunday dinner was a ritual carried out on Saturday night. Cutting coal and firewood was done in advance. It was not quite like that at home but only that which had to be done was undertaken on Sunday.

Moreia played a crucial and a central role in our development. This was our Cathedral and the deacons of that time were the big guns – the *"hoelion wyth."* Attendance at services three times every Sunday was the norm and I also remember attending the occasional prayer meeting that was held every Tuesday evening in the vestry. Many of the elders, and even some of the women, would go on their knees and gradually graduate from controlled sentences to more emotional outpourings and escalating to quite a *"hwyl."* This for me was not only fascinating but highly entertaining. It made quite an impression and I remember, when the opportunity arose, acting out what I had witnessed in front of a captive audience in school. The chapel would be very well attended every Sunday and the vestry would be full of children for Sunday School. There was a children's service every month and this was an excellent preparation for an aspiring future actor!

But there was one Sunday when I decided that Sunday School was not for me that afternoon and I conjured up a plan. Very often our dog Bob would follow me for a certain distance before deciding that it was time for him to go home. Well, this particular afternoon I encouraged him to follow me all the way. We reached the vestry a few minutes late, I opened the door and ushered Bob inside. Marged Walters, who looked after the chapel, was on sentry duty and immediately sent him out. I explained that I would now have to take him home. The plan worked out to perfection.

Easter would mean a new suit ready for the annual Singing Festival held on Easter Monday. I always looked forward to the "*Gymanfa*" and the rehearsals leading up to the big day since it provided an opportunity for me at a young age to eye the talent of the other chapels that joined in the celebrations. During one *Gymanfa* I thought that I was going to get my first ever kiss. Five of us lined up behind the chapel to wait our turn to sample the sweet lips of a certain girl from one of the other chapels. I was the last in the queue and I was confident that all that practice over several months with the hand mirror at home would stand me in good stead. But, alas, when it was my turn she decided that she had enough. It was devastating and her decision proved a hammer blow to my ego!

The *Gymanfa* was held in Moreia and Bethesda Ponthenri on alternate years. There would be three rehearsals before the actual *Gymanfa* with the guest conductor taking charge during the final rehearsal on Easter Sunday. The famous BBC broadcaster Alun Williams was one of those conductors and apparently it was his very first *Gymanfa*. His secretary for many years was Alma Carter (née Jones) who was a stalwart of Salem Four Roads. Alma later worked for the National Eisteddfod but unfortunately she died far too early. A delightful person and a dear friend, Alma's roots were deep and although she lived with her husband Ricky and son Rhys in Cardiff they also had a home in Meinciau. I came across this tribute to Alma in the July 2007 edtion of the *Dinesydd*:

> *Enaid tyner oleuni; enaid*
> *Oedd annwyl iawn inni;*
> *Enaid y mawr haelioni,*
> *A Duw oedd yn d'enaid di.*
> Robin Gwyndaf.

The Sunday School trip was one of the highlights of the year with around five to six buses carrying the excited children as well as the equally excited adults to the seaside.

The trip described in the Welsh section more or less depicted the type of outing experienced in my day.

Saturday meant watching Meinciau Rovers in action – the best team in the world! I simply could not understand why teams such as Arsenal, Manchester United, Spurs and Newcastle were not on the fixture list. My ambition was to play centre forward for my team and follow in the footsteps of Ivor y Black, Kerri Williams, Reggie Morris, Eric Beynon, Vernon Tŷ Cam and the other household names that graced the teamsheet. But Non (John Bowen), my grandfather, decided that it was time to broaden my horizons and one Christmas day he took me to Tumble to watch the home team play Pontyberem. It was the very first rugby match that I ever saw and I simply could not understand why there was nobody standing in the goals. According to the *Carmarthen Journal* over 3,000 people watched the match which Pontyberem won, thanks to a try scored by Ken Williams, the brother of Kerri and Maurice. It was the first time Tumble had ever lost at home to Pontyberem.

Christmas was always a special day. Every year old Santa would visit our house at least a week before he was actually due. He would leave the presents in the hatbox that stood tall in the passage. Quietly, without anyone noticing, I would investigate and wonder if he had remembered me again. No need to worry a pair of football boots and a leather ball there this year once more. Well done, Santa! But I would have to wait another week or so before these were handed over officially together with my *Eagle Annual* of course.

Christmas Day would finally arrive and the excitement was always overwhelming. The only downside would be the Christmas dinner because it always hindered my personal schedule of activities. All my life I have been unable to eat anything related to feathers and since my grandfather liked goose we usually had a goose for Christmas and on one occasion my mother hid a slice of goose meat on my plate amidst the beef, which is similar in colour. After eating most of what was on my plate Mama told me about the goose, resulting in my Christmas dinner seeing the light of day twenty four hours sooner than what it should have done!

Christmas morning activities would repeat themselves every year – out and on to the stadium, new ball, new boots and the thousands from all corners of Meinciau would fill the stands that stretched upwards towards the clouds. Every single one of them would be mesmerised by the genius from Torcefen. Even the cows appreciated the talent of this boy as he sidestepped their daily offerings! After another victory to Swansea Bay, the thousands would make their way home, the stands would disappear and the cattle would claim their rights and resume their wanderings around the field and graze in peace once more. Swansea Bay was the name of my imaginary team because of my affinity with Swansea I suppose, and I firmly believe now that it would be a far better name for the side known as the Ospreys. At least people would know where it is.

I had seen through the myth of Father Christmas a few years before I let on. Wyn Gwndwn Mawr, who was a few years older than me, tried to convince me once that it was all deceit. I knew very well that he was telling the truth but he did this in front of my parents and I had to convince them that I was still a believer, as I feared my presents would stop with immediate effect.

Before long I was old enough to accompany my grandfather every other Saturday to support the Llanelli Scarlets at Stradey Park. If Llanelli won, Non would be delighted and it would certainly ease the pain if he had lost on the gigis that week! It was the era of R. H. Williams, Henry Morgan, Wynne Evans, Cyril Davies, Ray Williams, Geoff Howells, Terry Davies and of course my hero Carwyn James. Howard Ash Davies was of that vintage as well and he lived for a while in Meinciau with his parents and brother in Hafod y Gân, a house built by Non on the lane leading to Gellygatrog farm.

Although Llanelli was and still is my team, in contrast to almost every Scarlet supporter I did have a very strong affinity with the Swansea All Whites. There is no doubt that this came about because I went on holidays every summer to stay with my Aunty Jean, Wncwl Jack and their son Gethin who lived at 7 Wordsworth Street, Mount Pleasant. Wordsworth Street was a cul de sac with a huge wall across the bottom of the street. There were very few cars around and, consequently, the street became our football field, our very own Vetch Field. Living in the house next door to the wall at the bottom of the street was Roy. He was about my age and we became big friends, playing football and cricket throughout the holiday. Roy was John Charles and I was Ivor Allchurch or Len Allchurch or Terry Medwin or Cliff Jones. But there was only one winner and that was always John Charles.

21

Years later another generation of children played on our (what was by now a reduced playing area) Vetch Field in Wordsworth Street, in the boots of John Toshack, Terry Yorath and Roy Evans. Little did the children realise that the stranger visiting number 7 to see his uncle and aunt and watching them play used to play on this very pitch with Roy; the Roy Evans who lived at the bottom of the street and who later went on to play for Swansea Town and Wales. Sadly, Roy is no longer with us. He was returning home from a game of football when he was killed in a car accident on the Heads of the Valleys road.

I remember very well one sunny afternoon. It was the beginning of the football season and I decided to go for a walk along Milton Terrace, a street that was perpendicular to Wordsworth Street. After walking about two hundred yards I reached a point where after climbing the wall I was able to see the Vetch and watch the Swans. I was too young to go to the match on my own but this vantage point satisfied my curiosity. The wall overlooked the gardens of the houses below. There I was settling down to watch what I could of the match when suddenly I was the victim of such verbal abuse that it would have put the terraces of the Vetch to shame. In the garden below, unknown to me until she had her tantrum, was this woman with her bloomers around her ankles answering the call of nature. I decided to make myself scarce and off I went and back to the safety of number seven.

Aunty Jean was my father's sister and her husband uncle Jack was well known for his sleeping exploits. He was a bus driver and since he did not have a car he travelled to visit the family in the Meinciau area by bus. On one occasion he went back to Swansea on the last bus. As usual he fell asleep but this time he did not wake up until the early hours of the morning when he found himself in the bus that had been parked for the night in the garage!

They had a coal fire in Wordsworth Street and since both of them were out working my aunt had tied the front door key to a piece of string behind the door for the benefit of any family member who wished to call or for the coalman to deliver the coal. On this particular day Uncle Jack was home, sleeping in front of the fire. It was the day that the coalman called with a ton of coal for number seven. He did not realize that my uncle was in the house so he got hold of the key and opened the door. He proceeded to carry twenty bags of coal through this terraced house passing my uncle forty times while he kept snoring away in his chair. After completing his mission, he pinned the delivery note and invoice on Jack's lapel and off he went.

New Year's Day was another special day – or New Year's morning to be more exact. The colliery hooters would welcome in the new year and then, early in the morning, soon after breakfast, I would meet up with my cousin David, who is now the popular landlord of the Red Lion, Llandyfaelog. We would start in Gellygatrog, work our way around the village singing in the New Year and end our marathon in Torcefen. The hit song was:

Blwyddyn Newydd dda i chi
Ac i bawb sydd yn y tŷ
Dyna yw'n dymuniad ni
Blwyddyn Newydd Dda i chi.

The money collected would then be shared between us. Girls going out singing was a practice frowned upon but, fair play, Audrey Ynys Fach and Janet Blaenpant ignored that piece of bigotry and went round the houses exactly as we did. All the singing had to stop by midday. Singing after midday could bring bad luck! Looking back over all those years I am positive that there was snow about more often than not and even if there was no snow the ground was frozen solid. Unfortnately, singing in the New Year is a custom that is fast dying out; we should endeavour to reverse this trend. In my humble opinion singing in the New Year is far more important to us as Welsh people than celebrating the imported Halloween. New Year's night invariably meant a family outing to Llangyndeyrn Hall to watch Edna Bonnell's drama group.

I remember electricity being installed in Torcefen – before that we had gas lighting with a gas cylinder in the kitchen. Until we had a proper bathroom we used to bathe in a sink in front of the fire, just as the miners used to do. The toilet was an outside building next to the old house opposite our back door. It was furnished with newspapers cut into squares for the customary ritual. I believe that some of today's papers would be very appropriate for that particular function!

Every summer also meant going on holiday with my grandfather to New Quay. We always had the company of John Jones, Gwndwn Mawr and his grandson Wyn. The two grandfathers were first cousins and great friends, although of contrasting personalities. John Gwndwn Mawr was a deacon and one of the pillars in Moreia. My grandfather was rather reticent with regards to religion, although I am sure that he was a firm believer in his own way. John Bowen Torcefen enjoyed the occasional pint or three and there were a few nights when the two men went their separate ways.

On one occasion they both decided to go for a swim in the sea, although neither could swim. In addition to that drawback neither had the proper attire for such an adventure and our bathers were out of the question. So, after a conference that must have lasted the whole evening, it was decided unanimously that we would all get up early the following morning and make our way to Traeth Gwyn, a secluded beach that would have no prying spectators. The next morning duly arrived and at an unearthly hour we made our way to Traeth Gwyn where the two Olympians stripped to their long johns and in they went. They had a whale of a time before they came out and after Wyn and myself had made a quick head count we trecked back to our guest house with two happy and contented grandfathers.

As I grew older I joined the Chapel's Youth Club (*Cymdeithas y Bobol Ifanc*) with the minister Rev. I. G. Davies in charge. We met in the vestry on a Thursday evening once a month. Every year a varied programme was arranged for us; a programme which included social evenings, guest speakers and the occasional trip. A visit to Rhyl stands out in the memory as well as a visit to Ninian Park to watch a match between Cardiff City and the Arsenal that included the famous Wally Barnes.

As a child I could walk into almost every house in the village without knocking. In fact, most of the doors were open anyway. One of the houses that I visited every day on the way home from school was Mam Tŷ Top's house. She was not related to me but she was known as Mam Tŷ Top by all the children. She was the mother of Will Brynbarre and great grandmother of my friend Delme. She was well in her nineties and I always enjoyed our conversations. I remember calling with her on the way home from school one day and whilst sitting opposite her, discussing earnestly the important events of the day, smoke appeared from alongside her chair. It was smoke from her pipe that she tried to hide. The old lady was a secret pipe smoker!

In the Meinciau news March 26th 1948 edition of the *Carmarthen Journal* there is the following reference:

Mrs Evans Tŷ Uchaf (this sounds posher than Tŷ Top*) received a gift parcel from HRH* Princess *Elizabeth on attaining her 91st birthday.*

Lydia Evans or Mam Tŷ Top went on to celebrate her 98th birthday.

There were always gypsies parked near Garn Ganol and as a child I was very wary of them. The Storom Hill twins Peter and Peggy Davies were no help in this context whatsoever. Peter, Peggy and myself were playing in the field alongside the road one day when we heard "*Cart y Gyps*" speeding up the road. We dived into the hedge and listened intently to the man and woman chatting. I did not have a clue as the conversation was in English but Peter and Peggy were older than me and, as far as I knew, they could understand English. Peggy explained that the gypsies knew that there was a little boy living in this farm and one day they were going to kidnap him. I was mortified and to make matters worse I was walking home from school one afternoon with quite a wind blowing against me. I did not hear the gypsy cart until it was almost alongside. It stopped and the couple offered me a lift. I could not run away so I accepted their offer. They kept chatting to me but I had no idea what they were on about and as they approached Torcefen the cart picked up speed. This was it! They were going to kidnap me and as the cart flew past the entrance I jumped off and did not stop running until I was in the house. It took me a few years to realize that these kind people had no idea where their uncommunicative guest lived.

In the late Spring of 1953 I had to return to the hospital where I first saw the light of day – the Priory Street Hospital in Carmarthen. Apparently my appendix was playing up and it was decided that I would be better off without it. I had to remain in hospital for around twelve days before they could get rid of me and as a reward for being such a brave warrior I was able to spend a weekend in Parc y Bocs, Kidwelly, with my Aunty Margaret, her husband Elwyn and my cousins Janet and Susan. But what really stands out was the fact that I could watch the FA cup final on television. Blackpool, inspired by Stanley Mathews, beat a Nat Lofthouse inspired Bolton by 4 goals to 3 in a never to be forgotten match.

It was in the autumn of 1953 that we had our first television, in time to see Wales beat New Zealand. Not many people in the village had a television then and consequently our house was quite crowded when there was something special on. The FA cup final meant that the parlour was full to capacity every year with Mrs Baldwin in the debenture seat. Mrs Baldwin lived down the road from us and as someone who came originally from Blaenau Ffestiniog she was an ardent football fan. Friends such as Ron Ynys Fach, Ron Blaenpant and a whole terrace of grown ups meant on one occasion that there was no room for my grandfather until the furniture was removed!

The only thing I remember about my first day in Gwynfryn School was a fight I had with Vivian Jenkins, Brondeg, brother of Peter and Ann. It was the custom, apparently, for the older boys to encourage new arrivals to have a go at each other. Obviously, this was the Gwynfryn underground at work and since Vivian and myself started on the same day we were sitting targets. I cannot remember who won – maybe I don't want to remember. However, not one of us had an offer of a professional contract and our boxing careers came to an abrupt end!

But education and Gwynfryn School deserves its own chapter.

The now redundant village pump and the modern bus stop.

Moreia Chapel

Moreia was a branch of Bethel Llangyndeyrn but the initial meeting place for the Baptists around Meinciau was at the home of Mr and Mrs Thomas, Y Fan. It appears that they met every Sunday at 3 p.m. from around 1812 to 1827 when they managed to acquire the Methodist Chapel in Meinciau. This chapel was built in 1815 by the Wesleyans on land given by a Mrs Chamfred but, due to the failure of that particular group, it became the property of the Calvanistic Methodists. Again this venture failed and it was bought for £60 by William Jenkins, a deacon in Llangyndeyrn, for the Baptists. With additional money, that amounted to £510, work was completed on the inside of the chapel, allowing it to be officially opened on Thursday, October 4th 1827.

In 1861 it was re-opened with a larger capacity and on August 27th and 28th 1886 the present Moreia Chapel was opened. George Morgan was the architect, a very prominent Welsh architect of the period, and as one walks towards the chapel the unpainted front with its three arches is very impressive. I am not certain who Mrs Chamfred was but when the new chapel was opened in 1886 it was on land leased for 99 years by the Stepney Estate, suggesting that Mrs Chamfred was, in some way, connected to the Stepneys.

It was believed that the Baptists, in general, were more open-minded than the Methodists but that surely is open to question. The occasional non-Baptist visitor to Moreia felt quite uncomfortable during a communion service and would often leave the service prior to the communion because he/she was not invited to participate. This continued well into the twentieth century and of course the full might of the righteous in our chapels would descend on any young unmarried woman member who had the misfortune to find herself pregnant. She would be summoned before the chapel deacons chastised and face the possibility of being thrown out of the chapel community. What would happen to the male responsible? Well, the misfortune had nothing to do with him!

THE MINISTERS

James Davies, 1827-1849

James Davies was Moreia's first minister. Born in 1768 and a native of Pembrokeshire he became a minister at Bethel Llangyndeyrn in 1819 where he baptised ninety people in fifteen months. In 1827 Moreia also became part of his ministry and here, in contrast to the previous twelve years, peace and calm reigned for a period before it was shattered towards the end of 1836 when a group of around fifteen decided to worship in Ponthenri. This led to the building of Bethesda but, before long, seven of the original fifteen returned to Moreia. The Mormon movement sprouted in the area in 1848 and although a number from Moreia joined the movement James Davies, although eighty years old, received many new members that particular year.

It was a year later that Harri Evans, a sawyer from Carmarthen, was invited to baptise a number of new members. The baptism was held in Pontantwn and it was felt that it would be too much for the elderly minister to cope especially as he lived in Rhydargaeau. However, nobody had conferred with James Davies beforehand but some how he found out. A large crowd, as usual, had gathered to witness the ceremony when an angry James Davies arrived on horseback. He saw what was going on and went home bitterly disappointed.

James Davies was a brilliant preacher and a wise theologian. Towards the end of his life he became blind. He died on May 16th 1860 at the age of 92 and was buried in Rhydargaeau.

John Williams, 1854-1859

According to W. J. Rhys in his book *Braslun O Hanes Moreia*, John Williams was similar to his predecessor in his missionary spirit. It was this that led to John Williams becoming a missionary later in his career. He grew up in Felinfoel and when twelve years of age in 1836 he was baptised in Adulam.

A Hymn Singing Festival for the area was started and organised around 1843. John Williams was ordained as the minister for Llangyndeyrn and Meinciau on June 8th and 9th 1854 and when he became minister he encouraged Bethel, Moreia and Coedybrain to establish a Christmas Day festival.

The Religious Census of 1851 makes interesting reading as the following extract written by Thomas Griffiths, the Vicar of Kidwelly Parish Church, shows.

> . . . *Lords day in this Town is but very little regarded as a day for spiritual worship (pub)lick houses are allowed to be open, and frequented during Divine Service. Publick (hou)ses are very numerous in this place, and even the Town Clerk keeps a . . . publick house. Often time on the Lord's day we are not only able to hear cursing and . . . once swearing in our streets, but frequently we see most brutal fighting, and . . . (n)otice taken therof by the authority of theTown. This is the cause why places(of wor)ship are so little frequented and religion so little appreciated and professed at Kidwelly.*

Kidwelly, apparently, was a place to avoid on Sundays! This census was undertaken eight years before the religious revival of 1859. The pubs were open and the above comments could not be confined to Kidwelly alone. How accurate the census was is open to question. The census return for the chapel in Meinciau names the chapel as Soar Minkau erected in 1837. It accurately states that it was used as a Day School. Present on that particular Sunday were 40 scholars in the morning (most probably Sunday School attendees). The afternoon attendance was 180 while the evening prayer meeting at 6 p.m attracted 50 people. The average for the year was: morning 70, afternoon 180 and evening 50. These returns were in the name of David Thomas, Van who was a deacon. There is no mention of rowdiness on the streets of Meinciau!

John Williams was an extremely competent writer and the editor of *Seren Cymru* persuaded him to write a series of articles entitled *Hanfod Crefydd* – The Essence of Religion. In 1859 John Williams began his work as a missionary in India. He spent twenty years as a missionary but his health was failing and he was forced to retire because of this in 1879.

He came home to Wales and he died in Swansea at the young age of 56.

Thomas John, 1860-1863

Thomas John was the son of John and Mari John, 'Llain-wen', Blaenconin, Pembrokeshire, and the elder brother of Owen John who was at one time the minister of Bethesda Ponthenri. When he was thirteen years of age Thomas John was baptised in Blaenconin. It is also noted that he received a Bible in recognition for reciting the most verses within a specific period of time. He made use of this gift by holding services on Sunday evenings for other children – younger than himself when their parents were in chapel. His parents died within a short space of time closely followed by his sister, the eldest of five children, thus leaving Thomas with the responsibility of looking after the others.

Both Thomas and his brother Owen followed their father and learnt the art of working with wood. However, on May 15th and 16th 1860, Thomas John was ordained as the minister in both Bethel and Moreia. It was the time of the Religious Revival and many were accepted as new members in both chapels. The capacity of Moreia was increased and the chapel was re-opened on October 21st 1861. The cost was £200. £160 was collected, leaving only £40 to be paid. The membership rose from 70 to 140 in the three years of his ministry. To double the membership speaks volumes.

He left Meinciau for Aberdare where he remained for fourteen years. In 1872 he published a collection of hymns by various people. In June 1874 he returned to Llandre, Llangyndeyrn. He married when he was forty years of age and had ten children. Between 1877 and 1882 he was the minister at Seilo, Tredegar before moving on to Ffynnonhenri and Rhyd-argaeau, where he remained for nineteen years, In addition, Thomas John did a spot of farming and after retiring in 1901 he kept a smallholding for twelve years at Ffynnoneiddon, Llandyfaelog.

He spent his last few years in Ferryside. He died on February 26th 1920 and was buried in Llangyndeyrn.

William Davies, 1866-1870
William Davies was the minister from 1866 to 1870. He was born in Nant y Glo, Monmouthshire, in 1839, the son of an iron worker and the oldest of five boys. Three of his brothers were also ministers while the youngest, Thomas Witton Davies, was an academic and became a professor in the Baptist College and later at the University College, Bangor. William Davies began his ministry at Witton Park, Durham. He was ordained in Moreia and Bethel on 7th and 8th of August 1866. He was of a quiet disposition and was deeply interested in philosophy and theology. From Meinciau he moved to Brierley Hill, Ebbw Vale, where he remained until

1877. For the next four years he was in Jarrow before finally moving to Llangwm, Pembrokeshire, where he remained for 27 years. William Davies died on September 13th 1925 and was buried in Noddfa, Abersychan.

William Jones, 1872-1882

William Davies was followed by another William – William Jones. He first saw the light of day in 1848 in Liverpool but he was brought up in Penrhyncoch, Cardiganshire. At 10 years of age William Jones was working in the lead mines near his home. Two years later he was baptised and in January 1871 he was accepted to the *Athrofa* in Llangollen. His first ministry was Bethel and Moreia, beginning in August 1872. It was during his ministry that Salem Four Roads was built and on February 18th 1880 William married Elizabeth Thomas from Kidwelly.

Towards the end of 1882 he moved to Eldon Street, London, but he only remained there for three years before returning to Wales and to the Treharris area. William Jones retired in 1923 and during his time in Treharris he baptised 580 people. He died on April 23rd 1930 at the age of 82.

Morgan Thomas Rees, 1884-1894; 1899-1935

M. T. Rees was the minister in Moreia for 49 years and the only minister to die in office. He was born on April 6th 1860 and when he was 15 years old he was baptised in Salem Chapel, Llangyfelach. He worked as a blacksmith in Craig Cwm Colliery near Craigcefnparc. In 1881 he went to the Llangollen *Athrofa* before being ordained in January 1884 in Moreia and Bethel.

Soon after starting his ministry he established and organised a temperance society in order to keep the young people occupied. M. T. Rees formed a Fife Band and it attracted twenty-four members.

On March 9th 1886 he married Sarah Ann Hughes, a shopkeeper's daughter from Penybont, Llangollen. They married in Tabernacl, Llandudno.

The new Moreia Chapel was opened on August 27th and 28th 1886 with 234 members. Whereas the old chapel, apparently, faced towards the west the new chapel was built facing the north. During its opening the weather was beautiful, the congregations very large, the preaching was forceful and £400 was collected during the celebrations towards the cost of the chapel, which amounted to around £1,200. The debt was soon

The deacons of Moreia, Salem and Seilo with M. T. Rees, early 1930s.

cleared and a new vestry was built later on to replace the old one that had become rather tired looking.

Before long M. T. Rees found himself with five chapels: Moreia, Salem, Bethel, Pisgah Bancffosfelen and Seilo Carway. This, however, became quite a strain and he decided that he would have to leave the ministry of Bethel and Pisgah. He and his wife decided to leave their home in Crwbin and set up their home in Green Hall, Four Roads.

In 1894 M. T. Rees left Meinciau and Four Roads and moved to Soar, Penygraig, and the induction took place on Easter Sunday and Monday. However, they only remained there for two years – his wife could not settle down in Penygraig and missed their home in Green Hall. When the members of Moreia got wind of this Mr and Mrs Rees were invited to come back and a service of welcome was arranged for Monday, October 2nd 1899, when they were received with open arms.

Amongst his achievements was the introduction of the Young People's Society in 1924. This could be as a consequence of what happened in the Meinciau Eisteddfod of 1923. More information on this incident can be seen in the chapter on the Eisteddfod.

One interesting story about M. T. Rees is the episode concerning a local couple, Margaretta and Owen Davies, who went to live in America.

Margaretta could not settle in her new surroundings and decided to leave her husband and return to Meinciau.

M.T. disapproved of this and insisted that her place was with her husband and consequently escorted her all the way to Liverpool and ensured that she was on the boat back to America!

The new vestry doubled up during the miners strike in 1926 as a soup kitchen which was greatly appreciated by those who benefited from this arrangement.

M. T. Rees remained as minister until his death in Llandudno on June 19th 1935. It was a fruitful period for Moreia when it witnessed a substantial increase in members from 302, when he came back from Penygraig, to 402 when he died. This undoubtedly testifies to the popularity of the man, his industrious ministry and his powerful preaching.

Herbert Davies, 1937-1939

Born in Pandy'r Capel, North Wales, Herbert Davies worked in the bank in London. But in 1931 he entered the college in Carmarthen and he was ordained in Moreia and Salem in July 1937. He soon got married and Herbert Davies and his wife lived in Blaen y Fan, the home of Phil Thomas. When Herbert Davies suggested that it would be a good idea for Moreia to build a manse for its minister, Phil Thomas gave a plot of land for that purpose. It was said that Herbert Davies was a keen boxer at one time and

Herbert Davies.

during one heated discussion he grabbed hold of a certain deacon and ejected him from the meeting. By the following Sunday the deacon was back in his seat and both were friends once more.

However, Herbert Davies and his wife moved in March 1939 to Birkenhead. In contrast to his predecessor his reign was considerably shorter.

D. J. Richards, 1940-1941

Before taking up the ministry at Moreia and Salem in January 1940, D. J. Richards was a minister in Builth Wells for seven years and in Emanuel

Llanelli for three years. Again his tenure was short and by the end of November he and his wife were on their way to Knighton and Betws in the old county of Radnorshire.

In that short time, however, D. J. Richards accomplished a great deal and in his first year he baptised 24 in Salem and 7 in Moreia. He proved to be a powerful and intelligent preacher and was diligent in his pastoral duties. Mrs Richards was a constant source of help and she was instrumental in every aspect of the chapel's activities. Over £300 was raised towards a debt during their short stay.

In 1940 Mrs Mary Ann (Nancy) Jenkins, daughter of Henry and Harriet Morris, Meinciau Mawr, presented the chapel with an organ that served the congregation until 1963 when the present organ was installed.

Dewi Davies, 1942-1949

In his book on the history of the chapel W. J. Rhys portrays Dewi Davies as a man who was destined for the pulpit. As a child he would preach on the banks of the river Gwyddil near Pencader with his sister acting out the role of the congregation. It was at this spot that he was baptised at twelve years of age. Following a stint as clerk to a local contractor he worked with a goods seller in Carmarthen before he turned his attention to becoming a minister and began his studies at the Carmarthen College of Theology in October 1930. During his four years of

Rev. Dewi Davies.

study he won the Dr Williams scholarship, to the value of £10 on more than one occasion.

His first ministry was in Treorchy where he was ordained in 1934 and soon afterwards he married Annie Rees from Pencader. They had one daughter named Gwenda.

In 1942 Dewi Davies became the minister for Moreia and Salem. During his ministry he baptised 76 in Moreia and 50 in Salem. He was the first minister that I remember and he was very popular and successful but again within six years he moved to Moreia, Llanelli.

T. Elwyn Williams, 1950-1957

Elwyn Williams was born in Holyhead, Anglesey in 1922. In March 2009 I had the privilege and the pleasure of meeting up with him again in his Haverfordwest home.

M.T. – What led you into the ministry?

E.W. – I attended Hebron Chapel, Holyhead although very early on I went with my friends to the Methodist Chapel, Ebeneser. But when I was thirteen I went back to the Baptists in Hebron. I began to attend all the services and I was baptised when I was fifteen. Then I felt that I wanted to go into the ministry and I was guided by the Rev. W. H. Davies. As was the custom at the time, the applicant had to sit the Union's examination. I succeeded and I went to study at Rhosllannerchrugog. When I was eighteen I went to the Baptist College in Cardiff to study for three years. It was an enjoyable time in college and I was a regular player with the football team.

M.T. – You then accepted a call to Mountain Ash.

E.W. – Well, yes! I accepted a call to Ffrwd, Mountain Ash which was in the middle of the valleys and an area quite different to that of Holyhead. But before starting my career as a minister I married Enid Evans in Hebron, October 1945. She was brought up in Hebron and we were baptised at the same time. It was important to have a wife who was a minister's wife – it made things much easier and of course Enid was a true minister's wife. Within two years Eleanor Môn was born. I remained in Mountain Ash for almost five years before accepting a call to Manchester. On the Saturday before preaching there on the Sunday I took up the invitation of the chapel's treasurer to see Stanley Mathews play for Blackpool against Manchester City from the directors' box. I remember him telling me that he was one of the directors of Manchester City football club and if I accepted the call he promised that I would receive a season ticket every year and would be able to follow every game, home or away, from the director's box. As a football person this was quite a temptation. But back in Mountain Ash I went for a walk along the riverside in the company of Rev. S. J. Leek one Sunday night and he said that it would be a mistake to go to Manchester. He went on to explain that the majority of the congregation in Manchester had their roots in Angelsey and Caernarvonshire and by now this influx was at an end and in conseqeuence the chapel could only go downhill. Therefore, my next step was Moreia Meinciau and Salem Four Roads.

M.T. – What impression did Meinciau make on you when you came here?

E.W. – Our move this time was from a mining area to a farming village, although Meinciau was in the centre of the mining area of the Gwendraeth Valley. We moved to the Manse and had a wonderful welcome from everyone. We had a lovely time and made life-long friends. I enjoyed going on my bike and helping the occasional farmer

Elwyn Williams.

during the haymaking season. It was during this time that we had another baby girl, Eunice Môn.

We came across a number of characters and one character that must be mentioned is Miss Margaret Walters. Her home was the Chapel's Vestry and she always kept a roaring fire and everyone in the vestry would sit in front of it. She would always give me a cup of tea and it was always necessary to warm the cup with boiling water before pouring the tea. When there was a baptism Miss Walters would carry buckets of hot water to warm the water in the baptistery – this in order to make the experience more pleasurable to the minister. I remember years later when I was a minister down in Pembrokeshire and travelling to preach somewhere in the Swansea Valley I decided to call to see Miss Walters in the Vestry. She was not there, so I went over to her home – where she slept. I knocked but could not get a reply. So I went back to the car but I decided to knock once more and this time she answered. Her health was not very good but I had to have a cup of tea and a cake and that was the last time I saw her.

Next door to the chapel was the Black Horse. But it was chapel people that frequented the Black and of course the Black family were faithful members and extremely kind to us in the Manse, as they were to everyone else. The inhabitants of Meinciau were chapel people and this could be seen in every service with good congregations every Sunday.

There was a row of whitewashed cottages on the square and Siop Ley was one of them. I remember Siop Ley with affection – it was a meeting point, as was the water pump opposite the shop and the nearby baptistery. The post office was a meeting point as well and there it was possible to have everyone's history!

The quarry was a place that offered work to a number of people and if it could speak it could recount many a local story.

Every Christmas night a *Gymanfa Bwnc* was held, but it was not popular with everyone because of the day on which it was held and unfortunately it disappeared from the year's activities.

M.T. – You were quite a footballer and you were offered a chance to turn professional and play for Cardiff City. Did you consider playing for Meinciau Rovers?

E.W. – I received many offers. But I'm afraid that if I had accepted the invitation many within the chapel would not have been happy.

M.T. – The situation would be different today.

E.W. – Yes – we live in a different world.

M.T. – Was it difficult to turn down the opportunity to play as a professional?

E.W. – I wanted to go into the ministry and the two did not go together. I played regularly for the college and also for Cardiff City Reserves. Playing was an enjoyment and nothing more but when I was the minister in Moreia the football field was next door to the chapel and of course I would have loved to have played but, there we are, at the time I felt it was best not to.

As a student I played for Cardiff College in a cup final in Bangor. I headed a goal to make the score 1-1 but one of the opposition managed to put the ball in our net. However, it went through a hole in the side netting. It was not a goal but the referee thought that the shot was a goal and so we lost by two goals to one. After the match one of our players got hold of the referee and told him: "Look you golliwog if I was closer to the river Menai I would throw you in!" In that particular game I was hit in my eye and it looked really bad. The following Sunday I was preaching in Hebron, my home chapel. The congregation had quite a fright when they saw the state of their young preacher and that was the last time for me to play.

M.T. – You continue to preach – what about the situation today?
E.W. – I still go around but what is the matter with us today? I have preached recently with only two in the congregation. It is difficult to create an atmosphere when the congregation is so small. A lot of the fault lies with the parents – not encouraging their children to go to chapel – the lack of discipline is obvious. I still have a lot of enjoyment, especially when preparing sermons. I see us becoming more as chapel goers than religious people and those who do not attend a place of worship, often see this.

In 1957 Elwyn Williams accepted a call to Calfaria, Penygroes – a mining village in Carmarthenshire and the family moved to live in the village. Six happy years were spent there and it was where Eleanor was baptised. Then came the invitation to become the minister at Groesgoch and Trefin in Pembrokeshire where Eunice was baptised. He then officiated at Login and Cwmfelin Mynach before moving to Adulam Felinfoel and Salem Llangennech where he remained from 1979 to 1998 when he retired and moved with his wife Enid to Haverfordwest, in order to be fairly close to their two daughters and their families.

Ieuan Gwyn Davies, 1958-1979
Ieuan Gwyn Davies first saw the light of day in The Manse at Pontlliw in 1914 but when his father, D. H. Davies received the call to Calfaria, Llanelli, the family moved to the town of the Sosban. His father baptised him when he was twelve years of age. He began to preach in the chapel and he trained at the Carmarthen Theological College before accepting a call to Salem, Senghenydd, where he was ordained on October 16th 1941. He married Winifred Thomas, Plas Gwyn, Croesyceiliog, in 1942. Winifred was an aunt to Dr Alan Williams, the former MP for Carmarthen.

In April 1945 he was inducted as the minister for Gwawr Chapel, Aberaman. He remained there until he moved to Moreia and Salem in 1958. In 1959 the new cemetery was opened on land given as a gift by Edgar Williams who was one of the deacons. In July 1960 Verina Davies, Maes y Delyn, retired after forty years of service as chief organist.

I.G. possessed a gentle personality and he was in his element with the youth of the chapel. The Young People's Society was very strong with

Children of Moreia during the centenary celebrations, 1965.

well attended meetings in the Vestry on Thursdays once a month. These meetings also attracted youngsters who were not members in Moreia and this fact surely says everything about the success of the society. It was a varied programme every year – a dinner in the Boar's Head in Carmarthen, guest speakers such as Abiah Roderick and the occasional memorable trip comes to mind. I remember a trip to Ninian Park, Cardiff, to watch the match between Cardiff and Arsenal with the famous Walley Barnes playing for the visitors. There were trips to Rhyl, The Cheddar Caves, Worcester and Bristol Zoo. Quite often it would be the young people themselves that would organise these outings – a wonderful experience and giving a clear indication of the faith and confidence that the minister had in the group.

Between September 19th–21st 1965 the chapel celebrated its centenary. The old chapel was renovated in 1861 and the present chapel opened in 1886 but the services celebrated the incorporation of Moreia in 1865 into the Carmarthenshire Gymanfa or Assembly of Churches. The Gymanfa was in existence before the formation of the Baptist Union of Wales in 1866. There were numerous services held over the three days that saw the chapel full to capacity. On the Sunday there was a very successful children's service, whilst the young people performed work by Rev. Trebor Lloyd Evans and a communion service with Rev. I. G. Davies officiating was held in the evening. There was a service held on Monday night with the former minister of Moreia, Rev. Herbert Davies, preaching while on Tuesday afternoon the special celebration service was held with I.G. presiding. The Rev. W. J. Rhys, brother of M. T. Rees, gave the large congregation the history of the chapel. A number of people representing the denomination and various chapels in the area also spoke. Former minister Dewi Davies and Rev. Inwood Jenkins, who was raised in Moreia, preached in the evening service which concluded the celebrations.

I. G. Davies remained in Salem and Moreia until 1979 when he retired and went to live in Ferryside.

Eirian Wyn, 1980-1990

Within a few months a new minister came to Moreia and Salem. He was Eirian Wyn a young and enthusiastic person brought up in Brynaman.

M.T. – What inspired you to go into the ministry?

E.W. – I was a member in Siloam Baptist Chapel in Brynaman and my uncle Jac yr Hendre always used to say: "You'll make a preacher one day." It was strange but on the day of his funeral I was reading in the service and I decided there and then that I wanted to go into the ministry. I was seventeen at the time.

Ysgol y Banwen was my first school and then on to the Waun Sec. Mod. before going on to Pontardawe Grammar School. Then, after deciding to enter the ministry, I went on the preparation course to the Baptist College in Bangor.

The college principal, Rev. D. Eirwyn Morgan, was preaching in Siloam one Sunday and, as was the custom with visiting preachers, he stayed in our home. He was told by my parents that I was dyslexic and when he returned to Bangor I was told off for not informing the college of the problem. By then I was in my final year and towards the end of that year I was given the opportunity of following a course that basically looked at the relationship between the Welsh language and dyslexia – Welsh being a phonetic language giving, possibly, an advantage to someone with the problem. But after five years in college the answer was "no". I was ready to be a minister of religion. The first call came to two chapels Hermon and Star in Pembrokeshire and I lived in Y Glôg at the foot of the Frenni Fawr. I followed the bard W. J. Gruffudd and then, after I had moved on, he came back as the minister.

M.T. – You moved to Moreia?

E.W. – Yes, and it is strange how it happened. Mam and Dad were not feeling too well and I used to travel home regularly to see them and on one occasion I decided to take a different route to Brynaman and travel through Meinciau. There was a man hitch-hiking down to Pontiets and I stopped and offered him a lift. The hitch hiker was John Lewis, the Secretary of Moreia at the time, and he suggested a Sunday in Moreia for me. I had to refuse since my diary was full. However, I received a telephone call from another chapel, releasing me from an appointment on a certain Sunday. I contacted John and informed him that I was available after all. It turned out to be a children's service with members of Salem there as well and it was on the basis of that service that I was offered the ministry of Moreia and Salem.

1980 was the year and a year later on August 13th my wife Helen gave birth to our daughter Fflur. We lived in the Manse and from our bedroom window we could see as far as y Frenni Fawr, a wonderful view. But in order to ensure the future financial stability of the family, Helen and myself decided it would be better to own our own home and consequently we bought 'Brynawelon' – a stone's throw from the Manse.

We as a family made good friends during that time and friends that are still friends today although, unfortunately, some have passed away by now, such as Lyn and Berry Morris.

It was a very active community and I remember very well doing a musical entitled 'Barabas' with the children and the youth of the area. The show offered a wonderful opportunity for completely inexperienced people to enjoy the experience of being on stage. Helen composed the music and T. J. Morgan wrote the script but of course there were changes and adjustments made during the rehearsals. Brenig Davies was Jesus, myself as Barabas and Elin Rhys was Mair Magdalen. People like Elsbeth Jones were instrumental in the show's success and it was performed in the various chapels around the area.

I remember taking the children with Steve Jones canoeing and they thoroughly enjoyed themselves. The children together with the young people were also taken to centres such as Langton in Pembrokeshire and Bala Bangor College.

A pop group called Boco was formed and Boco went on to win the *Cân i Gymru* competition and consequently represented Wales in the Pan

Celtic Festival in Killarney. The group was called Boco after the affectionate name the pupils have for Elsbeth Jones, deputy headteacher of Ysgol Maes yr Yrfa who, together with Helen, helped the group. Boco comprised of Helen on the Harp, Gareth Williams Piano, Lyn Jones and Catrin Treharne. It is interesting to note that every member of the group has maintained a keen and practical interest in music.

M.T. – *You were responsible for a football team as well?*
E.W. – An under 11 side and an under 16 team if I remember. Manhattan Marketing sponsored the team and their name, of course, was on the shirt – yellow shirts with green sleeves.

M.T. – *In contrast to the original Meinciau Rovers who played in green shirts with yellow sleeves. You were young at the time. Was this an advantage whilst being a minister of two chapels?*
E.W. – Of course, I felt that I was on the same wavelength as the young people for a start and I did not feel any different with the older members either.

M.T. – *How did your conjuring go down with the faithful, considering that Elwyn Williams decided not to play football for the village team because he feared that it could split the chapel?*
E.W. – No problem, at least no one said anything negative to me directly. In fact I use conjuring to deliver the Christian message whenever that is appropriate.

M.T. – *Where did the interest begin?*
E.W. – Seeing David Nixon on television when I was a little boy and I was hooked. Conjuring was also a help to combat dyslexia since I would often visit the library to find books about conjuring. In order to learn the tricks I had to read about them and this of course encouraged me to read. Years went by before I made my first public show. Peniel vestry was the location when I was the minister in Moreia and Salem and I believe that this brought some publicity to the chapels. A name was required for the Equity card and Eirian Wyn was not suitable because there was someone else with a similar name. Therefore, Eirian Rosfa was chosen after my grandfather's farm. Everyone knew him as Dan Rhosfa and my father as

Wil Rhosfa and therefore Rosfa was a suitable name to choose. I must say that God has been very kind to give me other skills that have allowed me to conjure and act as well – talents that helped to keep my head above water and also to keep me in the ministry.

M.T. – What do you believe is responsible for the substantial decline within our churches today?
E.W. – Television for one thing.

M.T. – Exactly, as it affects everything else.
E.W. – Precisely. The chapel used to be the centre of activity but not anymore apart from the occasional exception. Other things attract people nowadays. I also believe that the narrow mindedness of certain influential chapel people of that age left a negative effect on the generations that followed.

M.T. – What is the answer?
E.W. – To keep at it and win over the children and young people and to try and make the chapel play an important part in their lives.

M.T. – How does Eirian Wyn live his life now?
E.W. – I am a full time minister in two chapels in Morriston and I also preach in Salem, Four Roads, once a month and I must say that there has been a significant increase in the numbers that attend the services in Salem. I do some acting as well and some work as stage manager when the need arises while Rosfa is still busy. I also do the Welsh announcements in the Liberty Stadium for both the rugby and football. I am also the mascots' coordinator for the Swans. It means escorting the mascots to meet the players before each game. I am friendly with the players. In fact, Angel Rangel's sister and her husband have named their baby boy Eirian. Another pleasurable task is to interview the "Man of the Match" and organise a quiz after every game for the platinum and gold sponsors.

The Ospreys sometimes play on Sunday afternoons. I have explained that it is the ministry that will always come first but, as it happens, I only preach in the mornings and evenings in Morriston anyway. I have given the members a challenge– if I can preach in the morning, go to the match and then preach in the evening then it's possible for them to do the same thing. And fair play, a number of them do attend the Liberty matches by now. I was, at one time, the secretary of the Tae Kwon Do Club in Carmarthen – I was very fit at that time. There is plenty to do and, of course, there is the occasional journey with Helen to see Fflur singing.

M.T. – Diolch o galon Eirian.

Emlyn Dole, 1995–

Since 1995 Emlyn Dole has been the part-time minister of Moreia. He is the son of James and Mair Dole, his father was the minister of Hermon, Llannon. The family moved from Llannon to Harlech and then to North Carolina, USA, for two years before moving back to Harlech. Eventually, the family moved to Maesteg and Emlyn belonged to the first cohort to attend Ysgol Ystalyfera. He left school at sixteen years of age and became an apprentice carpenter in Maesteg. His father, in the meantime, had moved to Soar Llwynhendy but, instead of moving back west with his parents, Emlyn decided to stay in Maesteg and learn his trade. It was during this time that Emlyn showed considerable potential as a footballer and had trials with Bristol Rovers.

But Emlyn was intrigued by the pull of the pulpit and he followed a foundation course in Bangor University before studying and gaining a B.D. degree. This was followed by a three year course of study in Aberystwyth and it was at this time that he played football for Goginan. He was ordained as a full time minister in Pontlliw as well as the minister of his home chapel Hermon, Llannon. After a year and a half he gave up the full time ministry to become the full time coordinator for the South Wales Sunday Schools. He was based at Trinity College, Carmarthen. He remained, however, as the minister in Hermon although by now on a part time basis and he has continued in Hermon to this day in that capacity. Emlyn then joined the BBC as a producer where he remained for four years before working within the media for two years as a freelance. Following this he joined *Y Cyngor Llyfrau* in a marketing capacity, which eventually led to the opening of his own book shop in Cross Hands. It was during his work with *Y Cyngor Llyfrau* that he was appointed as part-time minister to Pisgah, Bancffosfelen. But following the demise of his marriage the shop

44

was sold and Emlyn became Youth Officer for the Nonconformist Independents.

He then returned to full time ministry as the minister for Capel Seion, Drefach. Emlyn, however, was not happy and comfortable in his role as a full time minister. He found it difficult to have a point of reference that working every day in another capacity would provide and consequently he decided that working as a full time minister was not for him.

In 1995 Emlyn Dole became a part time minister in Moreia which meant that he had a contract with two chapels; Moreia, and Hermon Llannon. In due course Caersalem, Pontyberem made it three chapels. Then in 2006 he married Gwenda Owen and Emlyn, who had been a prolific composer for many years, was now busily composing for Gwenda and her daughter Geinor. Geinor, singing the song composed by Emlyn, *"Dagrau Ddoe"* won the 2001 *Cân i Gymru* competition in Llangollen before repeating that success in the Pan Celtic competition in Ireland.

Emlyn is also very active with *Cwmni Theatr Cwm Gwendraeth* which has performed several memorable shows. Emlyn is also a recognised translator which requires a special skill and in 2008 he was elected as a County Councillor.

He enjoys his work as a part-time minister and he enjoys being in Moreia. He describes Meinciau as a very friendly and homely village. He even had this feeling when he first climbed the pulpit of Moreia. He regards the modern church as a place where people can socialise as well. Emlyn has organised Chinese, Italian and Wine Tasting nights in the chapel vestry. These nights are light hearted and enjoyed by everyone and they indicate, to some extent, the way forward. We need to thank Emlyn for his vision.

Emlyn Dole is a very busy person and he is adamant that his ministry benefits greatly from the various experiences he gains during his working week. He enjoys playing golf but only rarely does he manage to practise his golfing skills. But Emlyn is sure of one thing – he will remain in Moreia until he reaches the end. Emlyn is completely unassuming yet he breathes a breath of fresh air to an establishment that can, in general, be both introverted and extremely reluctant to change.

But in Moreia, Emlyn has an enthusiastic team. The present deacons are Kerri Williams (Financial Secretary), Dilwyn Jones (Treasurer), Delyth Davies, B.A. (Secretary), Arwyn Jones and Elsbeth Jones, B.A. The organists are Elsbeth Jones, Margaret Davies and Ann Wright while the musical directors are Kerri Williams and Elsbeth Jones.

*   *   *

The Future

The dwindling congregations of today is a reflection of the society we live in and this concerns me greatly as someone who was brought up in the village where Moreia played such a central role. There is a school of thought that Wales, by today, is a secular country. I do not go along with that theory because research has shown that the vast majority of the people in Wales regard themselves as Christians although they do not, necessarily, frequent a place of worship.

This positive situation should be the springboard for future planning. Many of the faithful ones will not contemplate closing their chapel but it is vital that a new strategy is employed that meets the needs of the modern age. If the chapels do not embrace this then they will become no more than relics of the past that have no relevance to society. That process, of course, is already happening. It is often the case that several chapels within close proximity with meagre congregations still endeavour and struggle to conduct their weekly meetings. It would be far better if these chapels came together. Preserving the different denominations is the curse of modern day worship. Why does not common sense prevail so that they all come together to form one strong church. There is a need for the church to move out and be active in the community.

What is needed is a clear vision and a strong confident but sensitve leadership. This would create stronger and enthusiastic centres of worship that would play a central role in the community to which they belong. Opinions should be sought from people who no longer attend places of worship and their comments and observations should certainly be taken on board.

What does the future hold for Moreia, Meinciau? At the present time, as is the situation in countless other chapels, the doors are kept open by the few dedicated people. Let's hope that it will again play a central role in the life of the community and that someone, one day, will feel the need to write its history over the next one hundred years.

Meinciau Eisteddfod

There was an extremely popular Eisteddfod held in the chapel every Good Friday from 1909 until 1923. Considering the fact that the great religious revival of 1905 had influenced so many people it is somewhat surprising that the Eisteddfod was held on Good Friday which was, and remains, such a holy day in the Christian Calendar. However, the Eisteddfod drew large crowds every year with queues of people waiting to capitalise on the comfort of a seat when the opportunity arose. This was the reason that the Eisteddfod had to leave its home after what happened in 1923. During that particular Eisteddfod a group of youngsters brought bottles of beer into the chapel which they in due course drank in the gallery. When the call of nature duly arrived they decided to use the empty bottles to relieve themselves rather than go to the toilet and consequently lose their seats to those still on their feet. The deacons heard about this which resulted in the Eisteddfod having to move out of the chapel. The following year it was held in Ysgol Gwynfryn and then in a marquee in the well-known Cae Garej, but unfortunately it soon fizzled out.

The *Llanelly Mercury* gave good coverage to the Eisteddfod and the first reference to it is 1909. In the Mynydd Mawr news there was this snippet of information:

> *Mr W. T. Rees is the recipient of many hearty congratulations on his recent successes as champion soloist, he having taken no less than three champion solo prizes in two days. Does this establish a record in this county? Great praise was given him at Bethel, Meinciau and Capel Seion and that too by different adjudicators.*

According to the Carway news seven choirs competed in the chief choral competition with Carway under its musical director Edmund Davies winning first prize. The Carway Ladies Choir also won in a competition of four choirs. Violet Gilbert was the conductor and she also conducted the children's choir that beat two other choirs. Olive Gilbert was second in the solo for girls under 14. Therefore, quite an achievement for the village of Carway but this, according to the *Mercury*, made the people of Pontiets quite jealous or at least some of them.

"Hen le bach felna yn ennill." (A small place like that winning).

The eisteddfod motivated and encouraged local talent in Meinciau itself. A group of people directed by John Thomas won the competition for a party of eight at the Mynyddygarreg Eisteddfod with their rendering of 'Llygaid y Dydd'.

'Cythraul y Canu' has always been apparent in the eisteddfodic circle. This has remained to some extent to the present day although, possibly, watered down somewhat by now. However, it was very much alive following the Ponthenri Eisteddfod of 1910 as can be seen in the following two letters in the *Llanelly Mercury*:

Ponthenry Eisteddfod

To the editor of the Llanelly Mercury.

Sir – Please allow me to contradict the report of the Ponthenry Eisteddfod of March 26th 1910. In the trio and champion solo competition it should have been stated that J. Brython Williams was the winner of both. Also that he won the champion solo at Pembrey on April 2nd.

I shall be greatly obliged to you if you will allow this to appear this week. I am
J. Brython Williams.

The following week's paper included this reply:

Ponthenry Eisteddfod

To the editor of the Llanelly Mercury.

Sir – Will you kindly allow me space in your worthy paper to state the truth regarding the champion and trio competitions at the Ponthenry Eisteddfod held on March 26th 1910.

The contradiction which was made by J. Brythan Williams,
Pembrey, and appearing in your last issue seems to mislead the
public as the above was only co-winner with Mr W. T. Rees, Cross
Hands, in the champion solo competition, and with Miss Lily A.
Stone, Mr T. G. Williams and Mr Walter Beynon of Pontyates in the
trio competition. I am

Walter Beynon, Evelfach, Pontyates

Serious business these Eisteddfodau!

The 1913 Eisteddfod included a competition for participants that had not won five shillings. It was won by Tom Rees of Pontiets. Carway won the children's choir, Carmarthen Youth the chief choral, Five Roads the ladies choir and Carway the men's choral competition. Dyfnallt adjudicated the competition for the chair which was won by Rev. D. Bowen of Capel Isaf, Brecon.

The Eisteddfod encouraged poets to enter other competitions, as well as the chair, very often in memory of people who had passed away such as the memorial verses to Maria Harries, Llwyn y Graig, in the 1914 Eisteddfod. The winner had entered under the pseudonym "Dan yr Ywen" Who was "Dan yr Ywen" I do not know, but his or her verses in memory of Maria can be read in the Welsh section.

The 1914 Eisteddfod was an outstanding success with a record number of participants as well as a huge crowd. *Y Maes Gwenith* was the subject for the chair and it attracted thirteen entries, including one from Canada. The 1914 chair is now in the possession of Rhyddwen Jones in Drefach. It was won by Joseph Henry and it has remained at the family home. Joseph was a well-known local poet and the adjudicator, Rev. D. Bowen, winner of the 1913 chair, was very complimentary of the winning poem "Maes y Gwenith".

Verina Davies, who later became one of the organists at Moreia, won the piano solo in the 1916 Eisteddfod and in 1917 twelve poems were entered for the chair on the theme 'Tŷ fy Nhad' – My Father's House. It was the time of the First World War and the 1917 programme (in the possession of Eileen Anthony Davies, Four Roads) reveals that half the proceeds from the Eisteddfod would be donated to '*Ein Milwyr*'– Our Soldiers.

The 1918 chair was won by Jac y Bardd from Cefneithin. Thanks to some clever detective work by Meirion Jones this beautiful chair was traced to a house in Cross Hands. Mr and Mrs Dai Davies had safe-keeping of the chair but their wish was for it to return to Meinciau. Jack y Bardd or, to use his proper name, Jack Jones was a miner who suffered from chronic pneumoconiosis which forced him to give up work at a comparatively young age. He gained a great deal of success at various eisteddfodau. Carwyn James, whenever he saw Jac, would always greet him: "Wel, Jac, siwd mae'r awen heddi?" – How is the muse today? The muse was rewarded in 1918 when Gwili, the adjudicator, praised all seven entries but it was Jac's entry that carried the day.

Eisteddfod Chair, 1914.

Another huge crowd witnessed Carway choirs winning the chief choral competition in 1920 as well as the children's choir. Gwilym Elli from Pwll won the chair. In the Ponthenri news regarding the 1921 Eisteddfod it stated:

The majority of the villagers migrated to Minke on Good Friday. It is pleasing to note the success of two of our local competitors namely Edwin Williams and T. R. Beynon in winning the first and second prizes respectively.

Edwin was known locally as Pencwm and he gained a great deal of success in local eisteddfodau.

The weather was terrible on Good Friday 1922 but there was wonderful competition in front of a very good crowd. De Valera, one of the dominant Irish political leaders of the twentieth century, was the subject of the *englyn* and the winning effort belonged to Daniel Thomas of Pontyberem.

Hudol arwr Dail Erin – a loriwyd
Yw Valera Erwin;
Holltwr blew a'i wyllt air blin,
Hwn garai Senedd Gwerin.

The Carway Choir won the chief choral under their musical director Edmund Davies who undoubtedly made an enormous contribution to his village. The chair went to Rev. D. H, Davies, Hermon, Conwil.

There is reference to the 1923 Eisteddfod with Megan Davies of Pontiets winning the first prize on the piano for under 12. An interesting comment by the author of "O Ben Mynydd Sylen" questions the suitability of Moreia as the venue for such a popular eisteddfod that always attracted a large number of people from the Mynydd Sylen area. Whether those comments had any influence in the decision but 1923 was the last Good Friday eisteddfod to be held in the chapel. Religious services were held from then on to commemorate Good Friday whilst the 1924 eisteddfod was held on Saturday night, September 27th, in Ysgol Gwynfryn and organised by the Young People Society to make up, possibly, for what had happened the previous year.

An eisteddfod was held for the children of Moreia during the 1940s in the chapel, but no beer bottles were found anywhere!

The Rebecca Riots

Meinciau did not escape the attention of the Rebecca rioters. The Rebecca Riots began because of an English law that was despised by the countryside people of West Wales. The many toll-gates found on the roads of South Wales meant that a great financial strain was imposed on local farmers. They very much opposed the high tolls which had to be paid on the local turnpike roads that meandered through the countryside. Farmers found that moving livestock to and from the markets, transporting essential commodities, such as cattle, food and lime had become highly expensive and quite often these tolls had to be paid more than once a day. There were eleven turnpike trusts operating around Carmarthenshire alone, including the Kidwelly Turnpike Trust which had Meinciau under its jurisdiction.

Thomas Rees, or Twm Carnabwth, who hailed from the foothills of the Preseli hills in Pembrokeshire, was the original Rebecca. There exists different versions of the reason why the name Rebecca was chosen. One explanation can be found in Genesis (24:60). Thomas Rees was a faithful member of his local chapel and the following verse could have provided the inspiration:

> *"And they blessed Rebekah and said unto her, Thou art our sister, be thou the mother of thousands of millions, and let thy seed possess the gate of those which hate them."*

Another explanation given is that Thomas Rees, who was a big man physically and a well-known prize fighter, decided to dress in a woman's clothes and it is claimed that only one woman, a tall and stout maid by the name of Rebecca, was able to provide him with suitable clothing. Therefore, Thomas became known as Rebecca when out on mission and his fellow rioters were also dressed as women. Groups were formed to attack and destroy the gates. The riots broke out in 1839 and lasted until 1843.

It was at Efail Wen, Carmarthenshire, that the first attack took place. The economic climate of the period was not very good and a series of wet winters, resulting in a succession of poor harvests, did nothing to pacify an increasingly discontented group of farmers. In addition, the mostly English speaking landlords imposed high rents and tithes to be paid to the local church. The tithes (or ten per cent) was based on the produce of the land. This could be corn, hay, or even fruit and wood. But after 1836 tithes had to be paid in the form of money and payment in kind was stopped.

In the Meinciau area the tithes were collected in the barn of my home at Torcefen. The farm was owned at the time by Rees Goring Thomas who was in the process of building a mansion on his farm Gellywernen near Llannon. He owned a great deal of property in the area and Gellywernen was attacked by Rebecca in 1843. At the time it was occupied by a Mr Edwards the tithe collector for Rhys Goring Thomas who was described as an absentee landlord.

What really sparked the uprising were the toll gates that abounded in the countryside. Turnpike trusts such as the Kidwelly Turnpike Trust had been established to repair and maintain the roads and the tolls were set up to gather money to pay for this work. The Kidwelly Trust had intended to link Kidwelly with Llandeilo, therefore enabling farmers in the upper Towy valley to bring their produce directly to Kidwelly and eventually to utilise the railway from Kidwelly station. However, the road only reached as far as "Pen Trympeg" the junction of the Llanelli–Carmarthen road between Meinciau and Blaen y Fan quarry. Trympeg is probably derived from the word 'turnpike' or the Welsh term '*tyrpeg*'.

On June 19th 1843 two thousand people marched into Carmarthen and plundered the much hated workhouse while two months later over three thousand supporters of Rebecca gathered at Mynydd Sylen to protest. There was a great deal of animosity towards Rebecca and her daughters as was expressed in a June 1843 edition of the *Carmarthen Journal*:

A few nights ago these vagabonds were at their work of demolition at Llandyssil where they completely destroyed the turnpike gate. They also paid a visit to Pembrey gate and on Monday night to Penllwynau gate on the Brechfa road both of which were entirely destroyed. We sincerely trust that the Government will take such steps as will put an end to this extraordinary combination of depredators who have, for so long a period, carried on their vile practices with impunity.

It was on the 4th of February 1843 that the first attack took place in the Gwendraeth Valley. Clwyd y Garreg, Kidwelly, was the target. Later on in the year, on the 4th of July 1843, the Meinciau gate which was located on the square between the Black Horse and Tŷ'r Gât (Penybryn) was destroyed. Gates were also destroyed in Pontiets and Mynyddygarreg and later on Rebecca returned to the restored gate in Meinciau and also attacked gates in Porthyrhyd and Llanddarog. The *Journal* also notes that at the same time gates were destroyed at Pontyberem, Kidwelly (two gates) and the gatekeeper at Castell Rhingyll was soundly thrashed. There was widespread damage to the tollgates and even Church in Wales clergymen were attacked on occasions because of the much hated tithes that had to be paid on demand to the Church of England, even though the vast majority of the people were Nonconformists. In Hendy, however, the gatekeeper by the name of Sarah Williams died in an attack. There is evidence that several of the rioters also passed as vigilantes and attacked, for example, local villains and fathers of illegitimate children. John Hughes of Tumble, known as Jac Tŷ Isha, led the Rebecca Rioters that attacked the Toll House and Gate at Pontarddulais on September 6th 1843. He was captured and was convicted at a Special Assizes at Cardiff and sentenced to 20 years deportation to Tasmania, Australia. Jac Tŷ Isha is thought to be the only Rebecca (leader) caught in the act of rioting.

Later on that year several rioters, including Dai Cantwr and Sioni Sgubor Fawr, were transported to Australia and the Government was forced to call a Commission of Enquiry to explore the grievances that had surfaced in the countryside.

Eventually in 1844 all the gates were removed since the authorities had to admit defeat and they never appeared again. The act to consolidate and amend the laws that related to the Turnpike Trusts in Wales was passed.

Education and Ysgol Gwynfryn

The history of education within the area is part and parcel of the history of education within Wales as a whole. During the middle ages a large percentage of the population did not receive any kind of formal education whatsoever. Only the children of the rich landowners were in a financial situation to attend any of the few schools that existed at that time.

Around 1699 schools for The Society for the Promotion of Christian Knowledge were founded. The teaching was in Welsh and English and the Society published the Welsh Bible. Apart from the teaching of the catechism and literacy the boys would learn arithmetic and the girls needlework, spinning and weaving. The schools were held in an assortment of buildings and Gruffydd Jones, Llanddowror, worked diligently for the society. However, he felt that the Welsh language did not receive the status it deserved within this organisation and consequently he introduced his Circulating Schools.

Gruffydd Jones, through these schools, made an enormous contribution to the education of the ordinary Welsh people. Between 1739 and 1768 there were 24 Circulating schools in the area with 1,310 students. Reading the Bible was the main aim and people of all ages, including children, would be the students. The schools were held mainly during the winter months since the work carried out on the farms during this season was not as heavy as in the summer. A team of travelling teachers would set up the schools and work with the students for up to three months before moving on and repeating the process in other areas. Meanwhile, they would have trained and developed people to act as teachers within those schools before moving on. These schools were located at various places including Llangyndeyrn Church, Tŷ Iets in Pontiets, Cilcarw, Gwndwn Bach, Capel Dyddgen, Parc Matho near Glyn Abbey and Laswern, a farmstead located between Gellygatrog and Capel Dyddgen. Unfortunately, due to the lack of money, the schools eventually disappeared but an environment was created where there was a demand for education by the people. Two different bodies filled the vacuum that appeared following the demise of the

Circulating schools. These were the Charity and Private schools as well as the Sunday Schools founded by Thomas Charles.

In 1822 a charity school was opened in Pontantwn by Evan Donald Evans. It became a very popular school but it later moved to Carmarthen. English was the medium of instruction in contrast to the Sunday schools where Welsh was the medium. Many of the Charity schools were tied to the church and were often referred to as National Schools. According to the census of 1861 Eliza Benbough, daughter of Edward and Elizabeth Benbough, once of Gellygatrog, ran such a school in Cydweli. Many of these schools were eventually absorbed into the state system, either as fully state-run schools or as faith schools funded by the state.

In the few National schools that did exist around the first half of the nineteenth century English was the medium of instruction and consequently very little Welsh was used. The Welsh Not was used in many schools to discourage the use of Welsh and to force the children to speak English. Any child heard speaking English would have a piece of wood attached to a string tied around his neck. The piece of wood would be marked with the letters WN and the child wearing it at the end of the day would be punished.

It was a turbulent time in Wales towards the middle of the nineteenth century with uprisings and violence breaking out in many parts of the country. Questions were asked in Parliament about the tendency of the Welsh to break the law, as was witnessed during the Rebecca Riots between 1839 and 1843. It was even thought that it was the Welsh language that was to blame and following a speech by William Williams, a Welshman himself and the MP for Coventry, a parliamentary report was commissioned on the place of Welsh in the educational system. In this report the Welsh language and the morals of the Welsh people were lambasted. This is the infamous report that became known as The Treason of The Blue Books. A huge storm blew up when the report was published in 1847 especially as the commissioners were considered to have overstepped their brief and commented on the morals of the Welsh.

In the parish of Llangyndeyrn there were four day schools in existence in 1847 according to the *Carmarthenshire Data Base*. The schools were the Church School in Llangyndeyrn, The Wesleyan School at Ffosfelin, the School at Moreia Baptist Chapel Meinciau, and Mrs Peters' private school in Pontiets. In addition, there was a Sunday School in Moreia and according to the report, there were eight teachers (all male) responsible for 30 boys and 33 girls under the age of 15, while 18 boys and 11 girls were over the age of 15. The teaching was through the medium of both Welsh and English and it was noted that 36 could read the Bible.

However, according to the Treason of the Blue Books, the provision for education in Wales was poor. It maintained that the Welsh language was a disadvantage and stated categorically that there should be a concentration on English in order to improve the moral as well as the material welfare of the people. But it should be remembered that it was three Anglican barristers from England who researched the situation that prevailed in Wales and it must be questioned whether they were competent to carry out the investigation. These are the comments that followed the visit of William Morris to the school in Meinciau:

Meinciau School

The master of this school, which is held in a Baptist chapel, is a member of the Church of England; he pays no rent He told me that he does not receive enough from his school to support him, although he has no family; his brother who is a carpenter at Merthyr, has frequently to send him money. He told me that he lived many weeks in December last on only two scanty meals a day; he could not speak English correctly. I saw the following sentences written in several of the copy books although the handwriting was good: "Time slides incensible," "Wise men consceal their own private misfortunes."

The scholars were mostly labourers, and (a few of them) farmers' children. There were no desks, but the scholars write kneeling on the chapel benches.

Feb 4 1847　　　　*(signed) William Morris*
　　　　　　　　　　　　　　Assistant

The books used were written in English while Welsh was the medium of communication. The teacher was 46 and he had taught for twenty-four years. He was a farm worker before embarking on a teaching career but there was no record of where he had been trained.

The 1870 Education Act stipulated that every child was to receive primary education and a number of schools sprung up in the Gwendraeth Valley as was the situation in the rest of Wales. The old Church School in Pontiets was opened near the present Gwynfryn Primary School fifteen years earlier in 1855. This school was set up through the generosity of Richard Jennings, Gellideg. A certain Mr. Davies was the first head-teacher and it was said that he was very good at hammering knowledge, especially when using his stick! He was followed by a Mr Lewis, Mr Howells and a Mr Jenkins but very little is known about these people.

Atgofion was published to commemorate the centenary of Gwynfryn School (1896-1996). *Atgofion* includes extracts from the log books that reach back as far as 1869 and it provides a taste of school as well as community life from 1869 to 1929.

Attendance was most important to the headteachers and there are numerous references to this in the log books:

23rd June 1869 – A decrease in the attendance. Many children at the Railway which was opened for mineral traffic today.

This refers to the railway station in Pontyates.

15th November 1869 – Carmarthen Fair day. Being also very wet made attendance very low. Was disturbed by children coughing.

21st November 1873 – Some farmers' children absent today – turnip taking.

October 1880 – At least 60-80 children regularly at home in the district.

December 1880 – The attendance officer called visited the neighbourhood and warned the parents to send their children to school, the beneficial result being that the average has risen to 113.2 and Monitors had to be employed to cope with the increase numbers in teaching the 1st class.

The children were sometimes 'bribed' to attend:

*10th May 1895 – Schoolchildren given a treat. There was a magic
lantern exhibition given free in the evening to the schoolchildren by
the Master. This has made a visible improvement in attendance.*

The headteacher's pay was dependent on the attendance as well as on
the examination results in reading, writing and arithmetic, under the guid-
ance of the Inspector for Schools (HMI). The terms were a payment of
two shillings and eight pence per year for every child that was present
200 times during the course of the year as well as being successful in the
examination. It would be lower if the attendance was not satisfactory or if
the children failed in their examination. In 1893 a complaint was made by
the headteacher:

*I do not intend to make any more entries in this book unless and
until I am paid for last years work by the Board.*

Until the passing of the Forster Education Act in 1870 the education
system was voluntary and this act was the first step towards establishing
a national educational system, funded by the government. In 1880 another
act was passed that stipulated that every child should be educated up to 13
years of age. Therefore, children from the age of 5 to 13 were now catered
for within a national system.

In 1893 the Parish Schools Board took over the responsibility for the
national school in Pontyates and the school became known as the National
School. Then in 1896 Gwynfryn was opened a few yards up the road from
the old school. The headteacher at this time was R. F. Mathews. His first
entry in the Log Book states:

*I, R. F. Mathews, commence as Master of this school find children
with few exceptions ignorant of English. Discipline very defective.
First class unable to write down 50,050. Pronounciation also bad.*

Until 1870 Education was not compulsory, as can be seen from the
following extract:

*19th April 1871 – Admitted a girl this week who was over 10 years
of age but had never been to any school before.*

Numerous references can be found to the punishment of children for various misdemeanours.

29th April 1870 – Punished several of the children for being late this morning.

6th December 1895 – Had to cane John Thomas Caegarw for coming behind a female monitor after being put by the wall and raising her clothes. The matter kept him home the remainder of the week.

March 1899 – A boy Edwin Williams severely punished for entering the girls playground.

Is this the Edwin Williams (Pencwm) that made such a name for himself later on in local Eisteddfodau?

The school could be closed for various reasons:

19th October 1896 – On Monday and Tuesday afternoon we closed school. Thanksgiving services at Minke and in the neighbouring Church.

16th July 1886 – School was closed yesterday as the Master was carrying his hay in.

28th November 1892 – The school opened today (Monday) as usual but as a few children suffered from Scarlet Fever only 88 were present, and in the afternoon Dr Bowen-Jones the District Medical Officer of Health came round and ordered an immediate closing of the school for a fortnight at least and then to see how the epidemic would be.

10th February 1893 – School was closed today as the Parish Annual Ploughing Match was held.

Concerts were organised and the children competed in the eisteddfodau:

15th February 1895 – The concert for the benefit of the scholars was a decided success . . . The rendering of the Cantata by the schoolchildren gave every satisfaction and made the desired good impression.

7th May 1897 – Children's choir successful at Cwmawr Eisteddfod.

Insights into what the children did in class:

28th August 1875 – Slow progress made in Geography and Grammar as many of the children understand but little English.

As happens, from time to time, in all sorts of work there is reference to a very sticky situation:

18th March 1896 – I regret to have to report hereon the insubordination of the Assistant L. A. Jones. It should have been entered before but I had hopes she would change. Whenever any complaint is made to her instead of submitting I am bullied till I leave the room. A report of this today will be sent to the managers.

Then, six weeks later:

1st May 1896 – Miss Jones allowed to resign.

The Log Books contain references to important happenings in the community, such as the arrival of the first car in the village in November 1910 when the County Architect visited the school. The two explosions in the Ponthenri mine in 1920 and 1924 are noted when some of the children in the school lost their fathers and brothers. In 1921 the miners were on strike and meals were organised for the children in need. Evacuees were sent to Gwynfryn during the Second World War:

13th Sepember 1941 – The Headteacher cleared standard 5 classroom in order to accommodate approximately 36 children from Mayhill Junior School Swansea. They had been at the Old National School since 23rd of May 1941 in charge of their own teacher Mr Bibby.

Gwynfryn teachers in the early 1920s with Evan John Davies, headteacher.

The following were headteachers from 1869 to the present day:

R. F. Mathews:	8th January 1869–27th January 1870
William Harries:	7th February 1870–23rd October1871
Thomas Davies:	26th December 1871–27th April 1894
Evan John Davies:	1st May1894–31st July 1924
Thomas Thomas:	1st September 1924–29th January 1947
Evan Caron George:	31st March 1947–31st December 1972
Dilwyn Roberts:	1st September 1973–1988

Graham Thomas was appointed as headteacher following Dilwyn Roberts' retirement but due to illness was unable to take up his duties.

Cerys Francis was then appointed as headteacher and she remained in office until she retired at the end of the summer term in 2010.

Due to the restructuring of primary education by Carmarthenshire County Council, Rhian Evans, the headteacher of Ysgol Carwe, has been appointed as the headteacher of Gwynfryn as well.

Ken Williams, Awelfan, attended Gwynfryn in the 1930s and his comments about his school days in Ysgol Gwynfryn are interesting:

"I remember walking to school every day summer and winter. It was not easy for a five year old to walk down to school in the morning and then climb back up that steep hill on the way home. Using the cane was part of the punishment and this happened regularly. The headteacher was a disciplinarian to the core. There was no time to waste on play – work was everything and many children would succeed every year in the scholarship and gain a place in the Gram, i.e. Carmarthen Grammar School."

My Own Recollections
In my time (1948-1955) Mr George was the headteacher and the teachers were Miss Davies, Miss Mollie Rees (later Thomas) Miss Glenys Howells, and Mr Ken Williams. It was a happy school and we respected the teachers. Next door to the school was Gwynfryn House, the home of Gertie Thomas, the widow of the former headteacher Thomas Thomas. We as children were very wary of Gertie. If a ball was kicked into her garden it was a pointless exercise to knock and ask for permission to retrieve it. Permission would invariably be refused. Consequently, it meant that we would sneak in and sneak out, hoping that Gertie would not see us.

I do not remember much of the classroom lessons – the memories of the work seems to have evaporated considerably. But, on the other hand, there are some things that remain vividly in the memory. Miss Davies was my first teacher and to me at that time she was an Amazonian in stature and possessed a gentle and kind nature. I remember the milk bottles being warmed in front of a roaring fire in her classroom during the cold winter days. The milk in the bottles had often frozen by the time they arrived in school but by playtime they were ready to drink, thanks to the heat generated by that grate. On a wet day the children's clothes were dried on the guard in front of the grate. I am sure that the teachers took advantage of this amenity as well. On those wet days we were supervised by the senior girls during playtime. I remember like yesterday being commanded together with a few others by two aspiring teachers, Medwen Jenkins and her friend Gill, to entertain the class by conjuring up stories. Medwen, who is married to Geoff Hewitt, was the daughter of Miss Jane Enoch, a highly respected teacher who taught in the school for twenty years.

From Miss Davies I moved on to Miss Mollie Rees who, after marriage, became Mrs Thomas, and again I remember very little of the work we had to do. Then, on to Miss Howells and it was in her class that I became aware of the pleasure of reading. On one occasion I felt the force of her hand because, during a class reading session, I had read on a few pages while one child was struggling to read out aloud. It was on to Mr Ken Williams after Miss Howells before reaching the summit – Mr George himself.

We sat in rows, two to a desk. That was the pattern, with exception of Miss Rees and Miss Davies – I cannot remember the organisation of those classes. As I grew older I can remember writing endless essays, arithmetic lessons on a daily basis, a little History and Geography but the main emphasis was on preparation for the all important scholarship. In the scholarship class, once one year had sat the examination, then the count-down for the following group to begin the scholarship marathon started! Scholarship day was a monumental occasion. It would entail catching the bus to the Gram (Carmarthen Grammar School) to sit the examination that would determine which school we would attend after the summer holidays. When the results came through a number of us had passed but, to me, what was really important was that my parents had promised a cricket set if I was successful. In addition to the cricket set it also meant that I could now play rugby in my new school, having been a Llanelli Scarlet supporter for a number of years. Sport was very important to me and it has remained so all my life.

Mr George was a great cricket fan and he taught me a great deal about the technique of batting and bowling – advice that I have never forgotten. We played cricket against Ponthenri, Carway and Pontiets in the summer and in the winter it was soccer against those same schools. Unfortunately, those games were only sporadic – the old scholarship ruled! I find it depressing today to see youngsters with no apparent interest in anything of value but wasting their time and ruining their lives hooked on drugs. There should be a way to channel these young people to take up sport or other worthwhile activities that could occupy them.

Once a year there would be the school trip and I remember one such outing very well. It was a trip to London on the train in the company of other schools from the valley. Each one of us had to wear a tag around our necks with the following words: "*If found lost please return to Paddington Station by 5.00*". I believe that we all got back home safely. School trips used to be enjoyable and relaxed affairs, in contrast to the situation today

Christmas celebrations, 1953.

when every trip has to be justified on educational grounds. The social benefits and the sheer enjoyment of these annual trips far outweighed the need to relate these one off occasions to the curriculum. There are plenty of opportunities during the year these days to take the children on educational worthwhile activities.

I also remember receiving, with all the other children, parcels from Australia. These parcels would include tins of fruit, condensed milk and other gifts. This was the period after the war when there was a scarcity of such things in our shops.

I was the only boy in the school having piano lessons. I was not for one minute proud of this fact especially with the lessons arranged for lunchtime on Wednesday afternoons when all my friends would be playing football on the yard. I am sure that my mother's ambition, as far as music was concerned, was to see me play the organ in Moreia. I did not come anywhere near that goal and by the time I reached the grand old age of twelve my piano days were over. My sister Margaret, however, took over the mantle with far more success than her brother. Mama was very proud of the fact that Margaret reached that elevated height and has by now been one of the organists in the chapel for many years. Although I can entertain myself on the piano to some degree I regret that I wasted the opportunity that was given to me during those early years. It was not the only opportunity I threw away but we can all look back and believe, with hindsight, that we could have been wiser.

The singing lessons would involve the whole school gathering together in Miss Rees' and Miss Davies' classrooms. The partition separating the two classes would be drawn back for these lessons which were on a regular basis, indicating that singing had quite a high priority in the scheme of things. I thoroughly enjoyed those sessions, enjoyed them too much on occasions because, as someone who was raised in Moreia Meinciau, I tended to sing with too much gusto and I was often advised to tone down.

The school concert would involve a team of parents erecting a well built stage; the partition would be opened and the two classrooms became our Albert Hall. These, as far as I can remember, were Christmas concerts and they involved every child in the school. Little did I realise then that the stage was to play a significant role in my life later on.

During my time in Gwynfryn I, together with a few of the other children, had to attend the clinic in the hall in Pontiets. My problem was my feet – they were flat and to rectify the situation I had to follow a set of exercises. I followed them religiously but to no avail since they are as flat today as they have ever been. Those visits to the clinic allowed us to mix with children from the other school in Pontiets and one girl in particular caught my eye. It was Margaret Rees, Tŷ Isha, but, even at the advanced age of ten, nothing developed from those encounters and Margaret eventually married Heddwyn Jones who is a cousin of my wife, Dianne.

From what I can remember of my time in Gwynfryn it was a happy carefree few years in a caring, friendly and safe environment.

The World of Work

As in every village in the Gwendraeth Valley many people from the Meinciau area worked in the mines that dotted the valley. The valley is at the western edge of South Wales Coalfield. The coalfield stretches from Carmarthen Bay to Mynydd Mawr along the Gwendraeth Fawr Valley. Meinciau is situated on the ridge separating the two valleys – the coal-mining Gwendraeth Fawr and the farming community of the Gwendraeth Fach. The two valleys are very different. The Gwendraeth Fach is noted for its rich red soil in contrast to the Gwendraeth Fawr although farming is prevalent in this valley as well. The difference between the two is essentially due to the geological nature of the land.

The expansion of the coal industry resulted in the growth of the villages along the Gwendraeth Fawr. Trimsaran, Carway, Pontiets, Ponthenri, Pontyberem, Cwmmawr, Drefach, Tumble, Cross Hands, Cefneithin, Gorslas and Penygroes all developed as a result of an influx of people moving into the villages to work in the coal industry. These "foreigners" came from, in general, the rural areas of Carmarthenshire and Cardiganshire. On the other hand the villages in the sister valley are much smaller although there has been housing developments recently in some of them. Even so, Porthyrhyd, Llanddarog, Llangyndeyrn, Pontantwn and Llandyfaelog are considerably smaller in comparison with their neighbours in the other valley. The ridge that extends from Llandybie including the Llyn Llech Owain area, Mynydd Llangyndeyrn along to Mynyddygarreg is home to the limestone rock that resulted in the quarrying for it in Mynyddygarreg, Cwar Blaen y Fan Meinciau, the Torcoed quarries in Crwbin as well as in Llandybie.

The town of Kidwelly is there to welcome the two rivers before they flow on to Carmarthen Bay. I felt that until recently Kidwelly and its council did not regard itself as a part of the Gwendraeth Valley but by today, and due to the positive influence of Menter Cwm Gwendraeth, I believe that this perspective is gradually changing.

Looking back to the pre Norman period forests covered the Gwen-draeth Valley. The original castle built by the Normans in Kidwelly was made of wood. But as farming became more important the forests gradually began to disappear. The rich limestone seam enabled farmers to use lime on their fields. Small cottage industries sprouted all over the area and coal was mined, although on a very small scale, in various places along the valley. There is evidence that coal was mined in the early sixteenth century for domestic use and also for the limestone kilns that existed. Iron ore was mined in the locality and the furnaces at Ponthenri and Pontiets were kept busy. There is evidence that the Ponthenri furnace was in use in 1611, while the Pontiets furnace came into existence in the eighteenth century.

Gradually the coal industry expanded and the rate of expansion increased greatly towards the end of the nineteenth century. The development of the canal system followed by the railways was instrumental in this expansion. The Kymer canal that linked Carway with Kidwelly was the first canal to be built in Wales. This canal was built between 1766 and 1768 by Thomas Kymer to carry coal from his mine in Carway to the harbour in Kidwelly and to be transported by ship to far off places. The success of this venture resulted in others like Earl Ashburnham building a canal from his mines around Penbre Mountain to Kidwelly The "Kidwelly and Llanelly Canal and Tramroad Company" extended the Kymer Canal from Carway as far as Cwmmawr. There were problems however with the canals due to the fact that the level of the water also depended on the tide and with the development of the railway system the age of the canal came to an end.

Within a century the canals became relics of the past. It was far more efficient and quicker to carry coal, lime, minerals and people by train. By 1869 the Burry Port and Gwendraeth railway linked Burry Port with Pontyberem joining the path of the Kymer Canal on its way. The final stretch to Cwmmawr was completed by 1886. It also connected with the Gwendraeth Valley railway at Kidwelly and it was extended through to Llanelli in 1891 where it linked with the Llanelli Mynydd Mawr line at Llanelli docks. Before the turn of the century the Burry Port Gwendraeth line was officially a goods line with nearly 95 per cent of its income coming directly from the transporting of coal. Eventually the general public could use the trains and in 1922 the Burry Port and Gwendraeth Valley railway became part of the Great Western Railway system. Passenger service continued through to the British Rail era. Eventually, however, there was an inevitable loss of passengers to the competing bus services. Unfortunately the Burry Port Gwendraeth line came to an end and the following announcement was made in the *Carmarthen Journal*:

British Rail (Western Region) announced that passenger train service between Burry Port and Cwmawr to be withdrawn on September 21st 1953. It was 13 miles long. The following stations and halts to close: Burry Port, Pembrey Halt, Craigion Bridge Halt, Pinged Halt, Trimsaran Road, Glyn Abbey Halt, Pontyates, Ponthenry, Pontyberem, Cwmawr. An alternative bus service operated by J. James and Sons Ammanford to replace.

It can be said that the development of the railway was crucial in the way it energised the coal industry in the valley. Following the end of open cast mining in the area the line finally closed in 1996.

The coal mined in Cwm Gwendraeth was of a high quality. It was anthracite coal, hard coal that shone like glass and was regarded as the best coal in the world. Its quality did vary somewhat from mine to mine but there was a great demand for it.

However, it was the coal to the east of the Gwendraeth Valley that really drove the industrial revolution. This coal was known as soft coal. This coal burnt much quicker and it was easier to light the fire with it and consequently more practical in the open fires that existed in every home. The anthracite, although harder to ignite, would produce greater heat.

There were numerous accidents in the various pits around the valley and many homes in the district lost a father, a son or a brother as a result of these often fatal and tragic incidents. One of those homes was Delfryn, home of Dai and Maggie Morris. They lost one of their children, Edward, in a mining accident in 1938 at the Dynant colliery in Tumble when he was only eighteen years of age.

The coal industry has by now disappeared, the mines have shut and the open cast mine of Ffos Las is now a playground for the punters of horse racing. Who would have thought a few years ago that the deepest opencast hole in Europe would one day become the wonderful attraction it is today attracting leading figures in horse racing, including the Irish jockey A. P.

McCoy. Opposite the race course is the Glyn Abbey Golf Course also created on the site of an open cast area.

When I was a pupil in Ysgol Gwynfryn between the end of the 1940s and 1955 the Meinciau children would catch the 3.10 p.m. bus home. But before that bus arrived the bus carrying the coal miners home from work would drop off a contingent of black faced men. This would be before the age of the pithead baths – many of them would have to do with a tub in front of the fire or out in the back if the weather was kind unless they had a bathroom.

The vast majority of the miners had an interest in gardening. I believe that there were two reasons for this. Firstly, the psychological need to work in the open air in contrast to toiling underground in the bowels of the earth every day and also the need to feed the family. Many miners lived in smallholdings keeping a few animals. My grandfather, John Bowen, was a quarryman, a miner, and a farmer in his time – quite an entrepreneur! He paid dearly for his exploits underground like so many other miners who suffered from the effects of the coal dust with many of them dying at a very young age.

During the early 1960s hundreds of people moved into the locality from the north of England and from Durham in particular. Most of these moved to work in the Cynheidre Colliery. This influx of people did not have a real effect on the village of Meinciau but it certainly had profound consequences in other villages and especially in the schools. According to Ysgol Gwynfryn's centenary book *Atgofion* the following figures give an estimation of the number of children from this influx who became pupils in the local schools:

School	Number
Y Tymbl	28
Trimsaran	78
Bancffosfelen	50
Carwe	85
Gwynfryn	29

There is no doubt that this had a great effect on the Welsh language. Many of these children, thanks to the effort of the schools, learnt the language very well but it was detrimental to the Welsh language in the villages themselves. Although a great many returned to Durham others stayed. It is said that love overcomes all obstacles and as a result a number of marriages have tied the two communities together.

There were nine shops in Meinciau at one time. Ken Williams remembers five of them back in the 1930s. I remember four shops, Siop Ley, Siop Sâr, Siop Bryndelyn and later on Siop Gorwel. There were two carpenters and one of them, Will Jones, also had the skill to double up as a blacksmith.

Harding Jones was a much respected carpenter who lived with his wife Ross in Tŷ Cornel. Harding had a very pronounced stammer which endeared him to everyone. Harding, occasionally, would take his time to finish an order for a customer. One such customer ordered a wheelbarrow but there was no sign of this wheelbarrow being ready for delivery. A year or two later the customer was celebrating the end of the war in the Black and as he walked home in rather an unsteady state Harding saw him and shouted:

"Your wheelbarrow is ready."

"Keep it," was the reply, "I'm too old to push it now!"

Years ago I remember the hedgerows along our roads being perfectly manicured. Each road had a person responsible for its hedgerows. Will Morris Evans (known as Will Brown), the eldest of the Meinciau Mawr children, was one of those conscientious people who were described as having a length of road to look after. Will was half brother to the surviving fifteen children of Henry and Harriet Morris. Joseph Jones (Joe Black), Thomas John (Black Horse) and Gwyn Morgan, Bryngwyddil, were others that I remember very well taking pride in their work and ensuring that our hedgerows looked so immaculate during the growing season. By today modern technology has taken over from the sickle but the upkeep of our hedgerows does not come anywhere near the days of the length man.

The village had a full-time tailor in John Teilwr father of Maurice, Ken and Kerri. His workshop was a shed in the garden of the Black Horse. There was another tailor in the village before John in the person of Jacob y Teilwr.

Christopher Reel and his wife Catherine kept a little shop in their parlour. Catherine was the sister of Marged Walters y Bryn and they lived next door to one another. Catherine was blind since childhood and yet she knew exactly where everything was in her shop and was able even to differentiate between cotton reels and shoe laces of varying colours.

Christopher, whom I vaguely remember, was an Irishman and the young girls of the village were, apparently, rather afraid of him. After Catherine's death he became an eccentric and an unkempt character. He kept a gun in the house in case he was attacked. It was said that when he was taken ill the doctors in the hospital found a half crown coin lodged inside the skin of his foot. Yet there was a generous side to Christopher Reel. He bought the piece of land, where the new bungalows are located in front of the chapel, from Sam Phillips, Blaenyfan, and donated it later to the youth of the village.

In the 1950s Danny and Glenys Phillips opened a petrol station in their new home at Gorwel manned by them and their children Delme and Lon for several years. When Meurig Williams' parents took over the business they also opened a shop there.

Looking at the census returns of the nineteenth century a large percentage of the men folk in the area were described as colliers. There was also a high percentage of farm workers and servants. Many of the women were farm servants as well. Many men were classed as lime burners and lime hauliers. There was obviously enough work and demand for butchers, stonemasons, blacksmiths and carpenters throughout the century. The occasional female was described as a dairy maid, labouring woman and as a washer woman. It is sad to note that quite often young children were described as servants working in various farms in the area and there were numerous people described as paupers especially in the 1841 census.

FARMING

In his play 'Buchedd Garmon', Saunders Lewis underlines the responsibility we have to look after and cherish what we have inherited and to pass that inheritance on to future generations. This is a personal challenge to each and every one of us. We are living in a world that is constantly changing and as individuals and members of society we have to respond to these changes. Meinciau is no different to any other society and changes within farming along the years is a good example of this.

Surrounding the village are farms that have sustained generations of families. In the course of time many of these change hands and as a result the history of the farms get lost in the process.

There were numerous smallholdings in the locality. Invariably these were the homes of miners who enjoyed keeping a few animals and consequently farming several acres as well.

These are the farms and smallholdings in the area:

Cae Gwyllt, Garnwen, Wenallt, Torcefen, Gwndwn Mawr, Pantyrynn, Berllan, Llwynbustach, Gellygatrog, Llwynyfilwr, Tŷ Cam, Cae'r Arglwyddes, Blaenyfan, Llwynffynnon, Meinciau Mawr, Blaenlline, Mansant Ganol, Mansant Fach, Mansant Uchaf, Mansant Isa, Mansant Newydd, Ffrwd Vale, Morning Star, Bwlchwythaint, Llancwm, Hengoed, Ffoswilkin, Penlan, Gwndwn Bach, Pantyparchell, Pantymeillion, Blaen Meillion, Pantgwynau.

A number of farms, smallholdings and even houses have disappeared during the course of time. Dwellings such as Pencerrig, Pant Hywel, Gwndwn Isaf, and Tŷ Bach (Kiln House) are no longer in existence. There were five Mansants in the area whilst Mansant Uchaf (which was the home of Delyth Williams, wife of the Rev. Brenig Davies) has had several names within recent memory. It has been known as Mansant Lloyd, Mansant Williams and even Mansant Ganol which was rather confusing since there was already a Mansant Ganol nearby.

Names of Fields

When a farm is handed down from one generation to the next within the family the history of that particular farm is protected. This can be seen in the way the names of fields are often preserved over the years but when the farm is taken over by someone else then there is every likelihood that the original names get lost.

Torcefen

The Schedule Document of 1846 and the 1842 Tithe map indicate that my old home Torcefen was a farm of 45 acres. Rees Goring Thomas was the owner and it was farmed by David Jenkins and his family. It is worth comparing the names of the fields after a span of over 100 years.

I have used, when appropriate, the spelling as seen in the The Schedule Document of 1846.

Cae Pistill Issa . . . . Cae Caegwyllt
Cae Pistill Ucha . . . . Cae Top
Cae Pistill . . . . Cae Cefen
Cae o Flan Tŷ . . . . Cae o Flan Tŷ
Cae Pheasant . . . . Cae Pwmp
Cae Pheasant Ucha . . . . Cae Gwndwn Mawr
Cae Pant Hwel . . . . Cae'r Hen Dŷ
Cae Pant Hwel Fach . . . . Cae Pant Hwel
Cae Pant . . . . Cae Pant
Cae'r afon . . . . Cae Draw
Waun Ucha ⎤
Waun Ganol ⎬ . . . . Y Waun
Brwyn Issa ⎦
Waun Fach . . . . Waun fach

In the course of time several fields were sometimes joined together to form one big field as indicated above. The three fields – Waun Ucha, Waun Ganol and Brwyn Issa form by the 1960s one field, Y Waun.

Torcefen as a farm no longer exists. The farm house has been renovated. The cowshed, part of which had been the old barn where the farmers of the area paid their tithes over 170 years ago, has been converted into a modern house known as 'Tŷ Mair' and many of the fields have been taken over by Gellygatrog. This has resulted in the names of those fields disappearing under the umbrella of 'Caeau Torcefen'.

The Welsh language has disappeared from many of these farms and consequently the old Welsh names for the fields are disappearing as well.

Gwndwn Mawr

The Rev. Thomas Gronow was the landowner of Gwndwn Mawr back in 1846 with a John Jones and his family as tenants. The names of the fields at that time were:

Waunbriwnog, Waun Gwndwn Bach, Waun Ucha, Waun Issa, Cae Issa, Caepotch, Gors ganol, Waun Fach, Gorse ffynnon, Gorse eithin, Cae ....*, Llain y Pant, Llain y Knwch, Cae flan tŷ, Cae ....*, Cae

Canol, Cae Pant, Cae Newydd, Cae Knwck, Cae Mawr, Waun brwinen issa, Waun brwinen ucha.

(* Difficult to understand the handwriting).

Forward to the first sixty years or so of the last century when the family consisted of John Jones (no relation to the John Jones of 1846), his wife Get, daughter Catherine, her husband Hubert, and the grandson Wyn the fields were:

Cae Stabal, Cae Eithin, Llain Pant, Cae Pencerrig, Cac Isa, Llain, Cae Pen Tŷ, Cae Canol, Cae Bach, Cae Banc, Cae Draw.

As can be seen only a few names survived and, as was common practice in most farms, some fields have been joined together to make one much larger field.

Today, Delme and Alison Davies farm Gwndwn Mawr and it is interesting to see how the names have changed once more with several fields indicating the location of the field, use of the field or the previous owner: Cae Gellygatrog, Cae Laswern, Cae Llwynbustach, Waun Torcefen, Cae Bwys Sied, Cae Bwys Tŷ, Cae Sgwar, Cae Big Bales, Waun Fawr, Cae Du, Cae Berllan, Cae Meic.

Blaenyfan

Dilwyn and Adeline Jones farm Blaenyfan and the names of their fields today are:

Cae Cwar, Cae Dan Tŷ, Cae Atgos (location of Atgos building), Cae Wrth y Mans, Cae Gorwel, Cae Awelon (these two fields are next to new houses built since the 1950s). Cae Fron, Cae Garage, Cae Gyps.

Sam Phillips and his family farmed Blaenyfan when I was a youngster and Audrey, the daughter, provided the names that they used at the time:

Cae Bach, Cae Mawr, Waun, Cae Fan, Cae'r Hen Dŷ, Cae Gerddi, Cae Du, Cae Plwmp, Cae Garage, Cae Hade, Cae Draw, Cae Garnwen.

Only Cae Garage has survived from the 50s. It is interesting to note the names of the Blaenyfan fields in 1846:

Cae Tu Hwnt R'heol, Cae Cwar, Cae Dan Domen, Coed Rifon, Cae.... Ar Tŷ, Cae Adlydd, Y Graig; Waun, Llaindre; Cae Sticill, Cae Eithin, Cae Canol.

Cae Cwar became fashionable again with Dilwyn and Adeline.

Garnwen
In 1846 Garnwen had the following fields:

Cae Thomas David, Ty'r Garw, Cae Newydd, Cae Wrth Tŷ, Waun Fach, Cae Banke, Gwndwn Gwyn, Waun Eithin, Cae'r Cwm.

When Eric Davies and his family took over the farm around 1960 the names that they had for the fields were:

Cae Bwys Tŷ, Cae Pella, Cae Tŷ Gwair, Y Garn, Cae Isa, Cae Bushes, Cae Canol, Cae Dan Garn, Waun.

Gellygatrog
In 1600 Gellygatrog house was described as being the *"mansion house called Gellygadroge"*. There were four hearths in the house in 1670 and it was the home to the Lloyd family at one time. This family were the descendants to Jenkin Lloyd of Blaiddpwll, North Pembrokeshire. Thomas Lloyd came to Gellygatrog and his brother came to farm Allty-cadno, Llangyndeyrn. Towards the end of the seventeenth century the Lloyds moved from Gellygatrog and the farm became part of the Browne estate. There is evidence that John Browne was the owner in 1750 but by 1846 the farm was owned by the Rev. Thomas Gronow of Cwrt Herbert Neath, while it was farmed by a John Rees and his family.

When Edward Benbough was in Gellygatrog in the 1850s the rent was 17s 6d. By 1910 the 163-acre farm was valued at £4,629. Eventually, the farm became the property of the Fitzwilliam estate.

The following fields were noted in the 1846 Schedule:

Waun rhinga ucha, Cottage and Garden, Llain, Cottage and Garden, Part of Graig, Graig, Cae Bach, Cae Tail, Waun rhinga Issa, Cae Llwyni Mawr, Cae Llwyni Bach, Cae Cwm Mantais Ucha, Cae Cwm Mantais Issa, Cae Gin, Cae Brandi.

In 1933 my grandfather William Thomas and his family came to Gelly-gatrog and they bought the farm from the Fitzwilliam Estate in the early 1950s. These are the names that I remember:

Cae Rhod, Cae Glas Uchaf, Cae Glas Isaf, Cae Tail, Cae Sgubor, Waun, Waun Bella, Cae Llwyni Mawr, Cae Llwyni Bach, Cwm-antais Fawr, Cwmantais Fach, Cae Lafrens, Cae Lline, Cae Llanarch, Cae Grôs.

As can be seen many of the names have survived while others have disappeared. The farm has remained within the family. When William retired his son Rhys and wife Jean took over and by today it is farmed by my cousin Elwyn and his wife Cheryl.

Tŷ Cam

In 1846 Earl Cawdor owned Tŷ Cam which was occupied by Daniel Williams. The Tŷ Cam fields in 1846 were:

Cae Pant y Tailor, Cae rhwng y ddau Dŷ, Cae yr Odyn, Cae Dan y Graig, Cae Glas, House & Garden, Garden Ynnis.

By today the fields are:

Cae Front, Cae Glas, Cae Bach, Cae Mawr, Cae Top, Cae'r Ynys.

It is Alan Lewis and his wife Julie who live in Tŷ Cam today. Alan was born in Tŷ Cam, the son of Vernon and Phyllis. Vernon was a keen sportsman having played football for Meinciau Rovers with his brother in law Eric Beynon, and cricket as well for the village team. Both Alan and his brother Lyn joined the Dyfed Powys Police Force. Alan followed in the tradition of several Meinciau boys and travelled to Tumble in search of a wife. His hunting skills were equally as good as his predecessors because he brought back a lovely wife in the person of Julie. They have two sons Richard and Stephen and although both taught for a while they also are, by now, members of the Dyfed Powys Police Force.

The 19th century has been described as the golden age of the horse and in some areas of Wales the farm would be known as a one horse farm or a two horse farm and so on rather than by its size in acres. If it was a three horse farm for example it meant that it would take three horses to plough that particular farm. I only remember one horse in Torcefen. The large farms of that period employed servants who slept in the farm stable but as farming became more and more mechanised the number of servants declined substantially.

When the mind wanders back over the decades to that time it is easy to realise that the life of the farmer has changed drastically. The majority of the farms in the area were small – Torcefen was typical of such a family farm of around 40 acres in total.

The main emphasis was on milk production but also important was the growing of potatoes, swedes, carrots and an assortment of other vegetables. I can vaguely remember the land girls helping out with planting and harvesting such crops as potatoes. The land army came into being during the war as it was essential to grow as much food as possible and this support continued for a few years after the end of the war.

I remember the cows being milked by hand and each cow had a name – very different to what the situation is today. Every cow by now has in its ear a tag bearing a number which is registered on the computer. Names like Daisy, Topsy, Harriet, Morfudd and Blodwen brought the cows much closer to one – though the same cannot be said of the bare, cold characterless number.

Then the milking machine came into existence when rubber pipes enveloped the cow's teats and the milk was sucked via a pipe into the bucket. The bucket was then carried into the dairy and cooled. As a child I would often sneak into the dairy and drink the milk before it was cooled and I simply loved it but obviously it is not recommended! I also remember helping my grandmother to make butter in Gellygatrog. My job would be to rotate the handle of the barrel containing the creamy milk until eventually it would turn into butter. This task seemed to last for hours and often result in painful blisters.

The milking machine was succeeded by a system where the milk was piped directly to the dairy. By today, however, the cows walk into a milking parlour to be milked. The milk tanker collects the milk from the farm – the old practice of the farmer carrying the milk in churns to be collected from the milk stands by the lorry is long gone. I well remember a few farmers in the area selling their milk directly to the local inhabitants. But whereas years ago farmers might have around twenty milking cows by today the large farms will have well over a hundred cows, with the very large farms milking hundreds of cows.

The rotational system of farming was much in evidence years ago since this, apparently, was very beneficial to the soil. A hay field one year might well be a potato field the next year followed by corn and cabbage and sprouts in succeeding years. There would be a local market for these products and the task of collecting swedes, carrots, cabbage and other vegetables for loyal customers could be hard work in a cold and wet environment. Gellygatrog for instance would sell their produce to customers in Ponthenri. Gradually, however, the demand waned as it became more convenient to buy in the large shops that were sprouting up everywhere.

With the advancements made in the production of fertilisers that contained nutrients at a level never seen before, it was possible to fertilise the soil to produce grass and hay of a very high quality. It is even possible by now to pump slurry directly from the slurry pit onto the field. One negative effect that the use of fertilisers had on the land was the fact that it often found its way into our rivers to the detriment of the fish population. This in turn resulted in a decline in the number of otters. But since many of these fertilisers have been outlawed the fish have returned and there has been a substantial increase in the otter population once again.

The corn and the hay harvesting could be described as social events as neighbouring farmers helped each other, often sharing machinery. Even the villagers themselves enjoyed helping out. The hay harvest in particular was much enjoyed by the children who were given tasks such as raking the hay or leading the horse that pulled the cart from one small hayrick to the next. These were dotted all over the field. The children were often given the responsibility of making sure that nobody was thirsty. Cider, beer, ginger beer and even wine made from the fruits of the hedges were available to the thirsty haymakers and a sumptuous meal was enjoyed at the end of the day, not forgetting the much needed tea and picnic in the shade away from the scorching sun during the course of the afternoon.

But this has long disappeared; silage and big bales rule today and it is the contactors with their expensive machinery that undertake the work, often working well into the night. It is common practice now to harvest two or even three yields from the same field in the period stretching from May to September.

The old binder which could cut the corn and tie it into a sheaf has long disappeared and replaced by huge combine harvesters. Every season had its own job in the olden days, with haymaking during June and July usually if weather permitted. There was quite a revolution when the tractor replaced the horse which in turn had replaced the oxen. The tractor was so versatile it could undertake all sort of work and consequently taking much of the physical strain off the farmer himself.

The farmer's life has been completely transformed – he, or someone on his behalf, spends a considerable amount of time in front of the computer by now. The small farms are disappearing often being taken over by larger farms as has happened for example to Torcefen for now most of the land belongs to Gellygatrog which has also taken over most of the neighbouring farms of Felindre and Llwynyfilwr.

There has been substantial housing development around Meinciau recently especially on Heol y Meinciau towards Pontiets and also on Heol Meinciau Mawr. This surge in house building is seen all over Wales with the result that a great deal of agricultural land is lost. On the other hand, it can also result in people moving into the village invigorating the community. Unfortunately, it can bring problems to the area as well.

BLAEN Y FAN QUARRY

The Blaen y Fan quarry was a long established quarry which supplied quarry products to the South Wales market for many years. It was located about half a mile outside the village of Meinciau on the limestone ridge that stretches from Llandybie to Mynyddygarreg. The surrounding landscape is of an undulating nature and of predominantly agricultural use. During its time of working the quarry was approximately 50 acres in extent and was a feature that could be seen for miles around. By today the rock that was Blaen y Fan quarry has been eaten away by the hungry and modern machinery leaving a new window that has opened up a new horizon. It was of great benefit to the community but also it brought great sorrow to several families.

Prior to his death in 1852, Thomas Williams was the freeholder of Llwynyfilwr Farm and a section of the quarry was part of Llwynyfilwr. The other section was part of the Fitzwilliam estate which owned a great deal of land in the area.

Farmers from a wide area and for many generations obtained their agricultural lime from the quarry. Roads were constructed using Blaen y Fan quarry products. There were 14 lime kilns in operation during the 1800s supplying the needs of the local farmers. Only a few remained by the 1950s.

The process of producing lime was quite simple. Intermittent layers of wood, coal and limestone rock would fill the kiln to capacity and set alight. After burning for a few days the finished product – the lime itself would be ready for collection.

For many years the quarry was only worked intermittently but from the 1950s onwards there was a sudden expansion in demand and gradually with more efficient and modern machinery creating better operating facilities the quarry was extensively worked especially towards the latter part of the last century. Over two hundred thousand tons was produced every year until a huge crater developed which has, by now, filled with water. It was a very well developed site with crushing and screening plants, a roadstone coating plant as well as an agricultural lime plant, storage buildings, workshops and a site office.

The increase in demand came from various sources. The development of the harbour in Port Talbot, The Llanelli Coastal Development Project, further development of the highways including the M4 motorway and the development of the oil refineries in Pembrokeshire together with the army camps at Manorbier and Penally meant there was a steady demand for quarry products at those locations. No questions were asked when supplies were delivered to the secret work carried out in Aberporth and Trecwn. It was a case of drive in and drive out!

According to Huw Williams, Blaenpant, who worked as a foreman in the quarry for over twenty years, there was a regular workforce of around 26 workers based at the quarry from around 1960 onwards. The quarry provided a great deal of work for local haulage contractors as the total tonnage extracted every year underlines. By 2004 the extraction of stone was more or less completed although it is claimed that well over a million tons still remains to be quarried.

Several were killed on the site, including my great grandfather David Bowen, who was killed in 1897 when blasting using gun powder. He was only 31 years of age. His brother-in-law, William Jones, Gwndwn Mawr, was also killed in similar circumstances eight years later in 1905. Included in the Welsh section is a poem composed by the Rev. M. T. Rees as a tribute to William Jones. In 1974 Ashley Jones from Four Roads lost his life aged 52 and six years later Dewi Rees, who was only 36 was killed whilst working in the quarry.

There were a number of accidents in the quarry that caused serious injuries. Harri Gravell, Mansant Fach, for instance, lost his sight when blasting.

By today the constant humming of the machinery, the never-ending to and fro of the lorries, the laughter and sometimes tears of the workers has ended. The quarry that has so much history is silent. Nature has reclaimed Blaen y Fan quarry and a large lake has drowned what was its treasure.

Blaen y Fan quarry is now a lake.

Sport

MEINCIAU SPORTS AND RECREATION CLUB

A committee was formed in 1969 and in 1970 three fields, amounting to six and a half acres, were bought by the club. A letter sent in March 1971 by Barrie Beynon, secretary of the Meinciau Sports and Recreation Club, appreciates the help that the club received from Danny and Glenys Phillips who had provided the fields, for a nominal sum of £1,000, where the Sports Club and park is now located. During that year a children's corner was created. Meinciau, since 1987, is in possession of a fine Sports and Recreation Club building and in the minutes of a meeting that took place in the Black Horse on March 10th 1980 the following people were elected:

President   –   P. R. F. Cotteril-Seadon
Chairman   –   H. McNally
Vice-President   –   K. J. Sellick
Secretary   –   Jeff Morris
Treasurer   –   Mike Evans

In this meeting various committees were formed. A management committee was set up as well as committees for cricket, badminton and entertainment. A tennis committee was also set up and this showed an admirable vision, with the club as an umbrella for various activities, thus creating a situation where it was possible for the community to work together in organising different events. This was in contrast to different factions within the same community doing their own things, completely oblivious to what was going on elsewhere. There was a lengthy discussion on the need for a new building to be built in the park. In the AGM held in the Vestry on March 3rd 1981 a soccer committee was formed with the Rev. Eirian Wyn as secretary. This led to the formation of an under 11 team as well as an under 16 side.

In a meeting held on September 7th 1981 Dai Clark was given permission to purchase Netball Posts – cost £40. This underlined the opportunities that were available in the village, for there was a football pitch and a tennis court as well. But the main objective was to build a sports hall and that was quite a challenge to such a small community. Various ideas were put forward to raise money including auctions, pig roasts, fetes, concerts and a 100 club was set up.

Meanwhile, the Meinciau Badminton club was the first badminton club from Wales to tour abroad. This first historic tour was to Switzerland where they played four games winning two and losing two. Bethan Beresford decided to liven up the proceedings one evening whilst the team was dining and went over to the juke box and played what she thought was Diana Ross. What came out was Demis Roussos – a singer that no-one in the party had heard of before. Two days later they actually met him and all this happened before he became a household name. Meinciau got in first! The team also toured Malta, playing four games, losing three and winning one.

Badminton became very popular and the team played in Pontiets Welfare Hall before playing eventually in the new Meinciau hall. Ironically, soon after moving to their new home the badminton team disbanded. However, before this occurrence the team in 1985 won the Section 1 and 2 of the Carmarthenshire Mixed Couples. The men won Section 3 of the Swansea League while the Swansea League Mixed Couples Section 3 was also won by Meinciau. Members of the Badminton team during that period included Dai Clark, Doiran Williams, Bethan Beresford, Hywel Lewis, Robert Thomas, Mary Wagner, Delyth Bowen, Angela Evans, Tony Peters, John Bowen, Dudley Hardy, Delme Thomas, Mike Rogers, Richard Lewis, Dr George Paul, Jeff Owen and Graham Thomas.

The contribution made by Lyn and Jeff Morris, Mike Evans, Derek Rowlands, Meirion Jones, Malcolm Evans, Ann Williams, Maurice Williams, Dai Clark, Huw Nichols, Mark Sadler, Mike Bowen, Islwyn Samuel, Kerri Williams, Barrie Beynon, Meurig Williams, Eifion Bennett, Maelog Morris, Ken and Margaret Sellick, Beryl Evans, Eirian Wyn, Monica Nichols, Pamela Lewis, Doiran Williams, Nancy Jones and Ann Richards was crucial in the struggle to have a sports hall for the village. The support given by Nance Y Black was absolute and most of the meetings were held in the Black.

*The plate by Harvey Thomas to commemorate
the opening of the club.*

In a meeting held on the 4th of June 1984 it was revealed that £30,000 would be the direct cost of the hall to the club and much of this was met by various Government initiatives. Building started in 1985 and the hall was officially opened on Saturday, 3rd of October 1987. A special plate by Harvey Thomas to commemorate the occasion was commissioned.

MEINCIAU ROVERS AFC

I have not really overcome the great disappointment of never having had the chance to play football for my home village. I played rugby for the Pontiets Youth team for a couple of seasons – playing for Carmarthen Grammar School in the morning, as did many of my peers, and then the youth in the afternoon. Josh Edmunds, Roger Griffiths, Randal Isaac, Michael Ayres Williams, Owen Todge Jenkins, David George Lewis, Heddwyn Jones and the late Keith Morris were my contemporaries who enjoyed and relished the unwise practice of playing two games every Saturday. This came to a stop when the school banned us from playing for outside teams. Later on I had the opportunity of playing in the West Wales league for Cefneithin before joining Porthcawl RFC. However, all this does not compensate for missing out on playing for Meinciau Rovers. The opportunity never arose as the story of this illustrious team unfolds in the succeeding paragraphs.

The story begins soon after the second world war when a group of youngsters got together to form a team. It was in the 1946-47 season that the first match was played away and the opposition was St. Clears. The players changed in the Santa Clara pub and the match turned out to be quite memorable for more than one reason. The St. Clears goalkeeper broke his leg and what is remarkable is the fact that the players pooled together and collected £21 for the unfortunate player. There was a report of the match in the *Carmathen Journal*:

> *On Saturday last (Jan 18th 1947) Meinke were the visitors to St Clears and a really good game was abandoned before the end when St Clears were leading by the odd goal owing to an accident to Donald Williams, the promising St Clears goalkeeper, who was unfortunate enough to receive a fractured leg below the knee. After attention by Dr D. M. Hughes he was taken to Carmarthen Infirmary.*

A shed was bought from the Prisoner of War Camp near Aberbanc and was located in the corner of the field opposite the chapel. It was used as the changing room for a while. Friendly matches were organised against teams such as Pendine, Llanmilo, Carmarthen Post Office, Penrhiwllan, Conwil and Ponthenri. The boys would travel to the matches in a taxi and would, of course, pay for the privilege themselves. There were only twelve players available initially so it was imperative that every one avoided serious injury.

There was a report in the *Journal* of a match that was played against Llansteffan on Saturday, March 12th 1949:

> *Llanstephan United visited Minke on Saturday and won by 5 goals to 1. The state of the ground did not encourage good football but some excellent movements were carried out by both teams.*

Meinciau had by now their own pitch but it was not Wembley by any stretch of imagination. Matches were played on "Cae Minke Mowr", a field adjacent to the chapel and cemetery. It belonged to Meinciau Mawr farm and a rental of £8 a year was paid for the privilege. There was a steady slope leading from one goal to the other as well as a gentle slope running from the touchlines towards the middle. However it was home and the boys liked it even if the feeling was not mutual when it came to the opposition, especially when it was cold and miserable with a howling wind or a dense fog! Before every match the boys would make sure that the pitch would be cleared of the daily offerings that the cow population would make during the course of the week.

The early games were all friendly matches but the information is very sketchy. However, a major step forward was taken in the decision to join the Carmarthen and District League in the 1949-50 season. A committee was set up to put the club on a more formal footing. Maurice Williams was the first Chairman although he lived and worked in London. Lyn Morris was the Secretary and Dai Lewis, Llwynglas, the trainer and treasurer. The team played in green jerseys with yellow sleeves, green shorts and green and yellow socks.

Within a few seasons the team soon established itself, participating and doing well in the West Carmarthenshire Cup known as the Mond Cup which was a keenly contested competition between, initially, clubs located in West Carmarthenshire. The cup was named after the industrialist and former West Carmarthenshire Liberal MP, Lord Melchett, or as he was better known, Alfred Mond. It is a cup competition that is still fought keenly today. The early team included boys such as Ashley Lewis and his brother Noir, Ivor Jones, Kerri Williams brother of the chairman Maurice, Reg Morris, Denzil and Harold Bevan, Bernard Beresford, Gordon Miles, Vernon Lewis, Lyn Morris, Dai Pencwm, Noel Williams, Mel Morgan, Danny Davies,Vince and Cliff Edmunds, Mel Baldwin and Raymond King – the Stanley Mathews of the team although Reg Morris was also an excellent dribbler of the ball. I was convinced as a child that Vernon Lewis (Vernon Tŷ Cam) with his powerful left foot could, with the wind blowing from the direction of the sea behind him, kick the ball all the way from Minke to Bancffosfelen! One of the mainstays of the team was the ball boy Brian (Cwlff) Lewis who grew up to be one of the characters of the village.

The teams that made up the league that first season were:

Pendine Military Detachment, Llanmiloe, Llanstephan, St Clears Mydrim, Pendine, Trinity College, Carmarthen GPO, Mynyddycerrig, RASC (TA) Carmarthen, Meinciau, Evans Motors Carmarthen, Ponthenry Reserves.

It is the match on Saturday 24th of September 1949 against Evans Motors Carmarthen that was probably the first fixture that Meinciau played in the Carmarthen and District League. The Carmarthen Journal noted that Evans Motors won the match 7-3 but corrected the result the following week declaring that it was Meinciau Rovers who actually won the match 7-3! Quite a start! The next match resulted in a 2-2 draw with RASC. Some of the results that first season were:

Meinciau 5, Pendine 1
Meinciau 2, Llansteffan 2
Meinciau 2, Mynyddcerrig 1
Meinciau 2, Llanmiloe 1
Meinciau 5, Range Camp 3
Meinciau 2, Ponthenry 0 (League Cup)
Meinciau 2, Trinity College 3
Meinciau 3, Ponthenry 3

The 1950-51 season was very successful. The team won the League as well as the League Cup beating Porthyrhyd 4-3 at Carmarthen Park. They lost, however, to Carmarthen Town Reserves by 4 goals to 2 in the first round of the Mond Cup in what the *Journal* describes as a "*. . . hurly burly cup tie*"

These comments appeared in the Journal about another game that Meinciau won that season in Llansteffan:

"*. . . the attitude of the visiting supporters also is to be deplored.*"

This following a report of the match as a very rough game!
A player that became very prominent that season was Bernard Beresford – a player that could be described as the John Charles of the side. Some of the results that season were:

Cardigan 3, Meinciau 1
Meinciau 8, YMCA Carmarthen 0

Meinciau 3, Llansteffan 1
(Match played in good spirits, according to the *Journal*)
Meinciau 6, YMCA Carmarthen 0
Meinciau 3, Porthyrhyd 1
Meinciau 1, Trinity College 0
Meinciau 10, St Clears 0
Meinciau 5, Range Camp 0

The 1951-52 season opened with a thumping 5-1 victory over Pontiets. This was followed by 2-2 draw against Trinity College before losing 3-1 away to Porthyrhyd. The matches with Porthyrhyd were always fiercely fought but away from the field of play a jovial spirit prevailed amongst both the players and the supporters. The Porthyrhyd girls attracted a lot of attention and one of the Minke stalwarts, Kerri Williams, even managed to marry one of them. Kerri and Joyce have celebrated over 50 years of married life and have a wonderful daughter, Gillian.

By January of the 1951-52 season Meinciau led the table followed by Cardigan and Porthyrhyd. The double was achieved over Trinity College with an emphatic 3-0 home victory. Eric Beynon scored twice and Reg Morris scored the other goal. According to the *Journal* the latter match was an excellent game. Llanmilo were trounced 6-1 in the League Cup semi-final at Porthyrhyd. Meinciau went on to win the cup beating Trinity College 2-1 in the final played at Carmarthen Park. Ivor Jones (Ivor y Black) had a game to remember scoring both goals in the process which resulted in the cup returning to the Black Horse headquarters for the second year running. Ivor's daughter, Pat, is the present headteacher of Ysgol Pont-henri.

Thomos John Williams, his wife Nance and their daughter Marie were running the Black and Nance, of course, was born in the pub as was her mother and daughter. Thomos John was a member of the committee and an ultra keen supporter. He was more than ready to offer advice to any referee that dared to penalise his beloved team. In one game Bob Jenkins, the referee from Carmarthen, decided that he could not tolerate any more of the verbals he was getting from the touchline and he decided to send Thomos John off the field in disgrace! Thomos John continued with his advice but this time from the other side of the hedge – out on the road. Both teams and the referee would change in the Black and wash in the communal tub or *sincen* but on this occasion Bob's clothes were waiting for him outside. There was no welcome in the inn!

There is also a story about Bob Jenkins sending Ivor y Black off the field during one match. The following week Ivor was driving his lorry and Bob Jenkins happened to be thumbing a lift near Pensarn. Ivor recognised Bob, stopped, and offered him a lift. The guest in Ivor's cab only wanted to go to Priory Street but Ivor decided to give him a far longer lift than Bob requested. He did not stop until he reached Peniel. "Now then," said Ivor, "walk back from here you bugger!" Thomos John and Bob Jenkins, eventually, became good friends but I do not know what the relationship was between Ivor Jones y Black and the man in black!

Anyway back to the end of the 1951-52 season. Meinciau returned to Carmarthen Park to face Ponthenri in the final of the Mond Cup. The *Journal* describes the game as an example of two different methods of play. Meinciau employed the kick and chase but it was Ponthenri that played the better football. Obviously, this paid off for Ponthenri since they won by 3 goals to 1. Kerri Williams scored for the Rovers while one of the scorers for Ponthenri was Vince Edmunds who was to join Meinciau the following season.

At that time training was not in the vocabulary. Players were naturally fit to some extent because of their work and they walked everywhere. Training really just involved lifting a jug of beer in the Black on the Friday night before the match and then discussion on the tactics for the match: "What about tomorrow, boys?"

"Up and under of course," and that was the end of the discussion on tactics. Most of the boys would work on Saturday mornings before meeting in the Black, down a pint and then change in the old slaughter house. Kerri Williams' mother Alice would always insist that her son should drink a pint of milk before the match. It seemed to pay dividends because Kerri always worked hard throughout every game.

Season 1952-53 started with a crushing 10-0 win in a friendly match against Carmarthen YMCA, suggesting another successful season awaited the team. By the end of October Meinciau headed the league with Porthyrhyd in second place, followed by Ponthenri, Cardigan, Trinity College, Llanmilo, Range Camp Pendine, Lowndes and Carmarthen YMCA. The YMCA team by now was a combination of the town team and YMCA. By January Meinciau still led the table winning seven of the nine games

League and Cup winning medals, 1951.

played and drawing the other two. What underlined their success was the fact that they scored 49 goals while only conceding 9. Bernard Beresford was again a giant in the team scoring profusely throughout the season, with one beautiful header coming from a corner in a match against the students of Trinity that Meinciau won by 4 goals to 2. They beat Ponthenri in the semi-final of the league cup at Porthyrhyd before winning the trophy for the third consecutive year after disposing of Cardigan to the tune of 4-0 in the final at Carmarthen Park. Meinciau apparently were by far the better team in the final and fully deserved the victory. Ivor Jones scored two goals while Vince Edmunds and Denzil Bevan scored the other two goals. This meant that Meinciau were the League and cup winners for three successive seasons.

No team liked playing on the notorious Meinciau pitch. It was exposed to the elements and on a cold day the home team would always keep the visitors waiting resulting in a frozen opposition before even the kick off. Fog was another factor and during one game the fog was particularly dense and everything went so quiet that it prompted the goalkeeper Mel Baldwin to ask the young Verdun Lewis, who was the ball boy, to go and see what was happening. Everyone had gone, the referee having abandoned the game a few minutes earlier!

Season 1953-54 was not as successful, although the trophy cabinet was not bare by the end of the campaign. Newcastle Emlyn had joined the league by now and there was a keen tussle at the top between the new arrivals and Porthyrhyd. Meinciau were a mid table team although they reached the semi-final of the league cup, losing 4-2 to Porthyrhyd in the replay at Ponthenri, following a 1-1 draw previously. Yet again, after a pulsating 5-2 victory over hapless Tumble, Meinciau showed what a magnificent cup side they were, reaching the final of the Mond cup after beating Carmarthen 3-2 at Porthyrhyd in the semi-final, with Eric Beynon scoring one and Bernard Beresford the other two. They went on to win the final by beating Porthyrhyd with Cis and Vernon Morgans playing particularly well.

Eric Beynon was integral to the club's success. He was a hard nugget on the field and as a child I was always glad to see that he was playing as he invariably caused chaos in the opposition's defence. Eric gave invaluable service to the club both on and off the field as he served for many years on the committee as well.

The 1954-55 season was the club's last season in the Carmarthen and district league. Porthyrhyd and Ponthenri decided to join the Carmarthenshire League that particular season and consequently Meinciau joined the second division of the Carmarthenshire League in the 1955-56 season. This league was stronger, with the first division being particularly strong. In the same division as Meinciau were Llanelly Steel, Pwll, Five Roads, Carmarthen Town Reserves (Carmarthen Town firsts were by now playing in the Welsh League), Corinthians, Llanelli A, BPA, Seaside, Tumble, Porthyrhyd and Ponthenri.

The season began brightly with Meinciau winning three out of their opening four matches. One result that stood out was the 12-0 demolition of BPA. Other results included victories over Pwll 4-2, Corinthians 4-0, Carmarthen 4-0, Five Roads 6-5, Porthyrhyd 3-1, Ponthenri 3-1, Llanelli A 10-0 and Tumble 4-3. By the end of the season the team finished third, having played 21 games in the league, winning 13, losing 7 with one game drawn. This was enough to gain promotion. In the Shield competition they lost 4-0 to Trostre (a very strong side from the first division) in the replay after drawing 2-2 at the first time of asking. They also lost to Mercury, another first division side, 5-2 in the Darch Cup competition. After beating Llanelli A 8-3, and Llanelli Steel 4-3 in the first two rounds of the Senior Cup they lost 4-3 to another first division, Hospital Rangers, in the third round after playing extra time.

Undoubtedly, the standard was substantially higher in this league, especially in the first division and now Meinciau was about to join them. But there was still one more game to play in the 1955-56 season and that was the Mond cup final against Porthyrhyd. This is how the *Journal* reported the game:

Meinciau 2, Porthyrhyd 0

Meinciau won the Mond Cup at Richmond Park on Thursday evening by defeating Porthyrhyd by two goals to nil. The strength of the winning side was in their inside trio Alan Lewis, T. Peck and Beresford. With more speed in defence and more craft in attack Meinciau deserved their win.

Therefore, the 1956-57 opened with the green and yellows fighting it out with the giants of the first division and what a way to start – a convincing 6-2 away win over Bwlch. The *Llanelli Star* noted:

Shock result in Division One was the defeat of mighty Bwlch by newly promoted Meinciau. There was no fluke about the new boys' win either. They ran their more experienced opponents off their feet and deserved every one of their six goals.

Victories over Llanelli Steel 6-5 away, and 4-3 over Dafen at home while an away draw 2-2 in Trostre was a commendable start and Meinciau soon found themselves second in the table. They did lose however by 5 goals to 3 in the first round of the Shield in Seaside and this led to a rather slippery slope in the table losing four consecutive games: Dafen 4-3, RAF 5-3, Mercury 3-1 and Trimsaran by 4 goals to 3. But following another defeat by 5 goals to 3 against Trimsaran there was a remarkable turn around in fortune. Seven games were won on the trot that enabled Meinciau to finish the season in third place. In addition the team reached the final of the Senior cup, losing 3-1 to Mercury. On the journey to the final at Stebonheath they beat Trostre 5-4 in a replay of the game abandoned at home after 35 minutes due to the weather. The semi-final against Carmarthen went to a replay as well. A 3-3 draw became a 2-1 victory at the second bite. Meinciau again reached the final of the Mond Cup, meeting Newcastle Emlyn in the final at Richmond Park. But holding on to the cup this time turned out to be quite a battle. In fact it turned out to be a series of battles, since it took three games to sort out the eventual winners. The *Carmarthen Journal* covered the three matches:

Mond Cup Final

NO DECISION AT CARMARTHEN

Meinciau 2, Newcasle Emlyn 2

At Richmond Park on Friday evening, April 26th, Meinciau and Newcastle Emlyn drew two goals all in the final of the Mond Cup. It was real cup final stuff with thrills, spills and goal mouth tussles. It was drama packed on drama.

A crowd of nearly 2,000 watched the game which was played under ideal conditions although there was a stiff breeze blowing.

It was not classic football, though it most certainly did not lack excitement and interest. The whole of the 120 minutes of the game was played at a terrific pace and no quarter was asked or given. Just before the 90 minutes was up the Newcastle keeper J. P. Davies was injured when he went up to punch a high centre. During extra time he stumbled about his goalmouth holding his side and evidently in great pain. It was clear from the start that Newcastle were the more polished side. They found their men with good ground passes, whereas their opponents were content to play "kick and rush" football, but it must be said that it nearly earned them victory.

It was all Newcastle in the first half with their short snappy passes. It was a different story in the second half for Meinciau turned on the pressure but the solid Newcastle defence held out grimly. During extra time the play swung freely to and fro and it was anybody's game.

The Meinciau inside right, Bernard Beresford, the former Haverfordwest player, should have bagged at least half a dozen goals instead of the two that he did get. He was given plenty of the ball and was if anything too selfish and on one or two occasions took the ball off the feet of his own forwards. Trefor Peck, the Meinciau inside left took some time to settle down and during extra time played in defence.

The Newcastle forward line was much more dangerous than their opponents and looked more business-like when they got going. Both wingers, Jim Jones (left) and Mike Jones (right) made fine runs down the touchline and were not afraid to "have a go" whenever the opportunity arose. Centre forward Cliff Jones (captain) was always on the move but was closely marked by Meinciau's attacking centre half Allan Lewis.

Newcasltle are fighting for the championship of the Cardiganshire League, while Meinciau are well placed in the Carmarthenshire League.

Newcastle kicked off and straight away inside right Jim Gallaway brought keeper Phillips to his knees with a powerful shot. Seconds later the Newcastle left winger Jones shot over the bar. Newcastle pressed hard and deserved to be at least two goals in the lead. Meinciau then switched defence into attack and left winger Peter Jenkins went near to scoring. The first goal came rather against the run of play. A tussle in the Newcastle goalmouth and a lob from their inside forward Beresford bounced over the heads of the Newcastle defenders and into the net. Beresford was probably more surprised than anyone. This lead was only held for a short while, for back came the border county side and a bullet-like shot from Cliff Jones was well held by keeper Phillips. Unfortunately he let it slip out of grasp and into the net. Then the Newcastle winger M. Jones beat three defenders, crossed the ball into the goal and centre forward Jones was there to crash it past the helpless keeper.

The Emlyn side held on grimly to this lead, but in the 75th minute Davies in goal punched out a shot from Beresford only to see him run in and head the ball over his head into the empty net.

During extra time both goals had narrow escapes but the score remained at two goals each.

STILL NO DECISION

Meinciau 2, Newcastle Emlyn 2

After 240 minutes of football between these two sides – a total of time in two games – it has still not been decided who will hold the Mond Cup for the next 12 months.

At Richmond Park on Tuesday evening both sides battled it out to extra time – but still no decision. They hope to play the second replay on Mon-

day evening, May 6th, but as the open season closes on Saturday, they will have to apply to the Welsh Football Association to do so.

MOND CUP FINAL
WON BY CARDIGAN LEAGUE CHAMPIONS

Meinciau 3, Newcastle Emlyn 4

In the second replay of the final of the Mond Cup at Richmond Park Carmarthen on Thursday night, May 9th. Newcastle Emlyn narrowly defeated the holders Meinciau after fighting back from a 3-1 deficit at half time.

By winning the cup Newcastle have brought off the Cup and League double.

As the game was played during the close season, permission had to be obtained from the Welsh Football Association and the proceeds were in aid of the West Wales Football Association Benevolent Fund.

At the end of the first half Newcastle were trailing 3-1 but during the second half they fought back with such determination that they had the Meinciau defence at sixes and sevens and thoroughly deserved their somewhat unexpected victory. The Newcstle defence was cooler under pressure than their opponents who were easily rattled by the fast moving, sharp shooting Newcastle forwards.On the whole Newcastle were the better side. They played prettier more constructive fooball and showed they were in a different class. Meinciau were by no means blotted out of the game for the first 20 minutes very little was seen of Emlyn.

Outstanding Player

The outstanding player on the field was Meinciau's inside right Allan Lewis who was the architect of many Meinciau raids. Trefor Peck (inside left), Meinciau's Welsh ATC international, who played himself to a stand-still had to leave the field just before half time to receive attention to an arm injury. He later returned and played on with his arm bandaged. Without these two outstanding inside forwards, Meinciau forward line would have been at a loss. Both keepers had hectic times for on many occasions the woodwork at both ends were hit. Ten minutes before the end the Meinciau keeper Islwyn Phillips collided with his left back Peter

Jenkins. Both received attention on the field. Phillips had to come out of his goal and centre forward Huw Evans took over.

Newcastle's win can be attributed to their wingers, Jim Jones (left) and Mike Jones (right). They were fast and dangerous and gave the Meinciau defence a harrowing time. The Newcastle forward line was well led by their captain Cliff Jones, although he was given a hard time by Meinciau's former Welsh League player, Bernard Beresford (cenre half). The game was fast and the result hung in the balance until the final whisle.

Meinciau kicked off and attacked strongly. They should have been one up after 20 minutes play when centre forward Huw Evans had a golden opportunity to head in a centre from the left flank. Instead he headed to his right winger and the move came to nothing. Newcastle were beginning to find their feet and there then followed a great deal of mid-field play. Exchanges were not really exciting and it appeared as if both teams were sizing one another up. After twenty minutes play the game came to life and there was five minutes of hectic, exciting football. It started when Newcastle put the ball into the Meinciau net but the goal was disallowed. From the free kick Meinciau attacked and a shot from centre forward Evans rebounded off the goalkeeper to the feet of Evans who hit it home. Newcastle worked the ball up to the Meinciau citadel where after a goal-mouth tussle Gallaway headed into the net. Straight from the kick off centre forward Evans fastened on to a ball inside the Newcastle penalty area and hit it in from an acute angle past the advancing keeper. The Meinciau centre forward Evans let his feelings get the better of him and nearly came to blows with Gallaway but the referee intervened.

Newcastle were trying hard to come on level terms and the Meinciau goalie did well to hold a header from winger Mike Jones. At the other end Meinciau centre forward hit the bar and minutes later Peck also hit the woodwork with a header from a corner kick. Shortly before the interval Meinciau increased their lead when a high lob from Allan Lewis deceived the Emlyn keeper and fell over his head into the net.

Spirited Side

Newcastle kicked off in the second half evidently outsiders for the cup. Then, to everyone's surprise Cliff Jones (centre forward) took a pass outside the penalty area slipped two men, steadied himself and let go a terrific drive which flew in off the post. Newcastle were a spirited side and threw everything into an all out attack. They came to level terms with another out of the blue goal when Jim Gallaway let go a 30 yard shot which hit the back of the net before the goal-keeper could move. The winner came with a goal by Jim Jones who after working his way down the wing scored a fine goal.

Cup Presentation

Before the cup was presented by Mr Bert Evans, Ponthenry. Mr Tom Phillips (chairman of the West Carmarthenshire Cup Competition) congratulated both teams on such a fine performance and said that it had been a real thriller.

It is the first time that the cup has been outside the Gwendraeth Valley district for nearly 20 years.

Presenting the cup Mr Evans said: "It may be a good thing that it is going outside the Gwendraeth area for it is beginning to be known as the Gwendraeth Valley cup."

Members of both teams were presented with replicas of the cup.

The 1957-58 season proved to be a disastrous one for the club. The team lost its home ground and consequently all the home games were played in Carway. By the end of December the team had only won one match out of the twelve played. They were bottom but one with only Trimsaran below them. They were at the receiving end of several hefty defeats, conceding, for example, 10 goals on two separate occasions to Llanelli Steel.

In contrast the following season 1958-59 started really well with the team winning its first twelve matches which included an impressive 7-1 victory over newcomers Bancffosfelen. By the end of December Meinciau led the table having won every game, scoring 53 goals with only 17 against. Unfortunately, this success only camouflaged the sagging spirit within the club as a whole. The fact that the home games were played in Carway evaporated the tremendous spirit that prevailed previously. Influential players left and by mid March the team only played four more matches, winning one, losing two, with one drawn match. I believe that the drawn match was the last game Meinciau Rovers played. Park United was the opposition and the score was 1-1. The journey came to an end and it was confirmed by the *Llanelli Star*:

Meinciau who won their first twelve matches and at one time looked near certainties for promotion have withdrawn from the Carmarthenshire League.

With that announcement the illustrious and wonderful story of Meinciau Rovers AFC came to an end.

The team, until the move to Carway had wonderful support. Two buses of supporters for instance would accompany the team on visits to Porthyrhyd. There were memorable derby games with Porthyrhyd as well as with Ponthenri. There were a few never to be forgotten Mond Cup matches with Newcastle Emlyn which attracted huge crowds. I also remember Carmarthen Park being absolutely packed out for various finals involving the team.

The club offered a great opportunity for local boys to enjoy themselves. There were so many who, to this day, will reminisce fondly about that period. Boys like the late Cliff Bach Davies who never gave less than one hundred per cent on the field of play. A number of boys went on to play at a higher level. These included Trevor Peck who played for Cardiff City and Portsmouth. Bernard Beresford and Alun Pancho Lewis who played for Llanelli. Alun was quite a sprinter and he competed in the Welsh Schools Championships at Ebbw Vale. His younger brother Verdun was a very talented player who also played for Llanelli and captained the side for many years. Verdun actually played a few games for Meinciau when he was only fourteen years old. In a match once played at White Hart Lane between the reserve teams of Tottenham Hotspur and Cardiff City two ex-Meinciau players were on opposite sides. Trevor Peck was in the Cardiff side while Verdun Lewis, who was on trial with Spurs, played for the home team. Quite an achievement for a team that played on Cae Minke Mowr.

Another player who made a name for himself was Peter Jenkins. When in Carmarthen Grammar school Peter used to play rugby for the school in the morning and soccer for Meinciau in the afternoon. He eventually concentrated on rugby and he played full back for Llanelli, Aberavon, Bridgend and Maesteg.

There were a number of players, not previously mentioned, who made a valuable contribution to Meinciau Rovers. Players such as Hubert Jones, Arthur Phillips and Elfed Owens were all fine players. A very prominent player was Malcolm Howells. With his ginger hair he was always conspicuous on the field and a tower of strength in defence as well as being a real threat in the opposition penalty area when the opportunity arose. Mel Baldwin was a fine goalkeeper and he was followed by Meirion "Boi" Jones, an equally good player. Meirion was the son of Joseph Jones or Joe Black as he was known to everyone. Joe was quite a boxer in his day and was well known for challenging the boxers circulating the local fairs. He fought under the name Joe Blake – it was posher than Joe Black! For many years Joe, who worked for the council, was also the local grave digger. Other players who served the club well included another very good goalkeeper Islwyn Phillips, brother of Arthur, Huw Evans, Tommy Thomas and Gordon Miles. Iori Rees, an ex-Ponthenri player, joined the Rovers for a season before leaving for Mynyddcerrig. The demise of Meinciau Rovers coincided with the emergence of two neighbouring teams. Several players joined Bancffosfelen and Carway and until this season both those teams were still flourishing members of the Carmarthenshire League but, sadly, Carway has by now disbanded.

Under 11 and under 16 teams were organised by the Rev. Eirian Wyn during the 1980s and during the mid 1990s a Meinciau team once again joined the Carmarthenshire League. Mark Gower, who originally comes from Mynyddygarreg, and Huw Evans from Croesyceiliog were the instigators behind this venture, but unfortunately the village failed to embrace and support the team to anywhere near what had been the situation before. Boys from as far as Penygroes and Cross Hands played for the team but many of these youngsters, as they gained experience, moved on to play for teams higher up in the league. There was a need for more support and understanding and consequently the team folded. This was a great pity because having a football team was good for the Sports Club and for the village and the facilities were there in complete contrast to the previous set up.

The facilities are still there of course. By now rugby has grown deep roots in Pontiets, and although Ponthenri and Carway are nearby I believe that there is room for a football team in Meinciau and for that football team to rekindle the glory days of the past and to create and build its own history – and under the name of Meinciau Rovers AFC.

MEINCIAU CRICKET CLUB (MCC)

The MCC is a cricket club that is famous all over the cricket playing world. But in Cwm Gwendraeth the MCC means either Mynyddygarreg Cricket Club or Meinciau Cricket Club.

It was in 1933, apparently, that a team was first formed in Meinciau but it was two years later on the 27th of April 1935 that a meeting was held which resulted in a committee being formed. Garwyn Morris was named as captain, Bill Lewis vice-captain and Gwyn Thomas as secretary and treasurer. Those three also had the responsibility of choosing the team. The unemployed and boys under the age of 16 were expected to pay three pence every fortnight. This sentence was included in the minutes:

"That no fixtures be made if they have not got tools"

Most probably this meant that all the right equipment must be available – wickets, bats, balls and that the team should be dressed appropriately. In a meeting that was held on the 7th of May 1935 it stated . . . *"That the captain, secretary, Joe Morris, Gwyn Thomas, Gwyn Williams, Wynford Evans David Lewis and W. D. Williams be at the field at 6.30pm on Wednesday to make a new pitch."*

The team has played on various pitches around the village during its lifetime– two fields on the Mansant road, a field near the Halfway Inn, the field below the chapel cemetery which had a ditch running through it and finally, since 1972, the games have been played on the present ground alongside the Sports Hall.

In a meeting held on the 21st of May 1935 it was decided that the whole committee would pick the team enabling more people to have more power. Following a meeting held on July 1st 1935 the caretaker was dismissed from his position ". . . *being unable to give satisfactory service . . .*" and he was given five shillings for his services. The position was offered to Dai Morris for payment of £1.10.0 with ten shillings for being the storeman until the end of the season.

It was quite an enlightened committee because in the annual meeting held on the 17th of December 1935 it was decided to invite Dai Davies of Glamorgan County Cricket Club to give a lecture to be held in Ysgol

Gwynfryn. The club also organised a raffle and the first prize was a stand ticket and the train fare to see the Grand National in Aintree.

It was evident that cricket was serious business as the team members were in training as early as the beginning of April. There was quite a rivalry between them and the team down the road in Pontiets: *". . . no member of the Pontyates Cricket Club of 1935 be allowed to join"* – April 29th 1936. That statement could be looked at from two angles – no member could join because it would weaken Pontiets or there simply was no welcome for anyone who had played for the enemy. In my bones I think the latter explanation is closer to the truth.

By 1936 there was a cup competition in place. Games were arranged against Laugharne, Crwbin, Bancffosfelen, Whitland, Penbre, Cwmgwili, Ponthenri, Tumble, Carmarthen Post Office and Carway. The 1938 fixture list also includes games against Ammanford UAB, St Clears, Cynheidre, Cefneithin and Carmarthen Electric Supply. With the outbreak of war in September 1939 the cricket came to an end but the balance sheet for 1947/48 showed a profit of £45.3.3 which included money in hand from

Meinciau Cricket Club, 1936.
E. Beynon, E. Beynon, W. D. Williams, C. Rowlands, W. D. Anderson, W. Lewis.
R. Davies, G. Morris, D. D. Davies, W. Evans.
N. Gillesby, I. Jones (Capt.), R. Rosser.

1946/47. During 1947/48 money was received from membership, collections during matches, sports and a concert.

BALANCE SHEET 1947/48

Receipts	£	s	d	Expenditure	£	s	d
Membership	4	17	6	Cricket Kit	16	3	9
Collection on field	5	17	3	Football Kit	12	0	9
Sports August 16th	35	9	9	Fares paid by club	5	14	0
Concert Jan 3rd 1948	19	0	0	Present Maurice Williams	2	4	10
Total	£65	4	6	Badges	2	4	0
				Affiliation Fee	1	3	0
				Insurance		10	0
Carry forward from				Stephen Jones	8	0	0
1946/47	30	6	0½	Washing of cloth		3	6
				Postage and Phone	1	3	1½
Cash in hand	95	10	6½	Sec Expenses		9	6
May 1st 1948				Total	50	7	3½
Cash in hand	95	10	6½				
Expenditure	50	7	3½				
Total	45	3	3				

This shows how generous the cricket boys were in buying kit for the football team as well.

In 1949 the Llanelli and District Cricket League was formed but we have to jump to the 1960s to find further information about Meinciau Cricket Club. The 1950s were barren years as far as cricket in the village was concerned. It is possible that the success of the football club during that period more than satisfied the appetite of the locals. On the other hand, it could be petticoat power, with the wives and girlfriends having their way over the summer making up for the winter Saturdays!

From 1964 onwards there were friendly matches against Pendine, Cefneithin, Carway, Burry Port, Five Roads, Pontiets, Ponthenri, Bancffosfelen, Laugharne, Abergwili, Cydweli, Drefach and the occasional works and pub team. It must be said that record keeping on occasions was not always what it should have been! Prominent players of that period were Ieuan Morris, Vernon Lewis, Malcolm Evans, Michael Jones, Meirion Jones, Verdun Lewis, Dai Clark who was very active for the club over a long period of time, Jeff Morris, Barrie Beynon, Kerri Williams, Harry McNally, John Lewis, David Edmunds, Allan Williams, Derek Rowlands, Doiran Williams (who played a few games for Llanelli), Ronald Morgan and Brian Rees.

Peter Jenkins, a fine full back in his rugby days, and Alun Pancho Lewis also played for the village but these boys together with Alun's brother Verdun went on to play for such teams as Pontyberem, and Llanelli, a team that Peter captained for sixteen seasons. Peter, who was an all round sportsman, also played for the Welsh Secondary Schools team. Peter was a brilliant captain and a fine batsman as well as being an excellent bowler and close to the wicket fielder. In the book *The History of Llanelli Cricket Club*, Dyfrig Roberts describes Peter Jenkins as a volatile character: *". . . one who always called a spade a spade, and, if he had something to say, whether it was on the field or off it, he would definitely say it, and he wasn't particularly bothered whom he offended."*

However, with age, Dyfrig Roberts thinks that Peter mellowed considerably. Peter Jenkins made a huge contribution to Llanelli Cricket Club and this contribution was recognised when he was made a life member of the club. Peter's sons, Alfan and Steffan, followed in their father's footsteps and played for Llanelli and in addition also played for the Welsh Under 15 and Under 19 teams. Alfan played for Ynysygerwen in the village cup final at Lords. Steffan, while with Dafen, played for the Senior Wales team against Ireland, England and Scotland. Peter, Alfan and Steffan have all won the Dan Radcliffe Cup (the South Wales Premier Division Trophy) with three different clubs – Peter with Llanelli, Alfan with Ynysygerwen and Steffan with Ammanford. Meinciau can also boast that three village boys captained three South Wales League teams in the same season – Peter Jenkins with Llanelli, Allan Lewis at Pontyberem and Trevor Peck at Tumble. Steffan also toured Australia with a team representing the South Wales Cricket League and he was also a member of the Welsh under 15 and under 19 Rugby squad.

Meinciau Cricket club can be very proud of the Jenkins Brondeg family. Vivian, Peter's brother, played for the other MCC club in the valley – Mynyddygarreg but Vivian made more of a mark on the rugby field, having played for both Pontyberem and Kidwelly Rugby Clubs. By today he can be seen hitting a decent ball (most of the time) at the Glyn Abbey Golf Club. As far as I am aware their sister Ann never distinguished herself on the cricket or rugby field but her speciality was folk dancing and she has encouraged countless children to take an interest in this activity as well as in sport. She was, for many years, a schoolteacher in the Pontypridd area before returning as a Primary School headteacher to her county of birth.

But let us go back to Meinciau Cricket Club and the occasional one sided game, such as the match with the Square and Compass, Pontiets, on June 21st 1965. It may have been the longest day of the year but the Square and Compass innings was remarkably short! They only managed 8 runs in reply to Meinciau's total of 105 for 5. Michael Jones knocked 77 of those runs while Vernon Lewis took 7 wickets for 5 runs to demolish the pub side.

By 1972 Meinciau, thanks to grants from the Welsh Sports Council, had a proper cricket ground and this opened the door for them to join the Carmarthenshire Cricket League. A great deal of work was undertaken to convert the three fields to a proper cricket ground. By joining the league it was necessary to have quite a strong squad of players to compete in the league as well as playing a number of friendly matches. By this time players like Leighton Morgan, Will Morgan, Mark Sadler, Maelog Morris, Alan Rees, Keith Jones, Clive Thomas and Joe Wyatt had established themselves in the team.

Carmarthenshire League games could be long drawn out affairs played over 40 overs but the friendly match played against Porthyrhyd on 8th of August 1974 was short lived. Porthyrhyd batted first and scored 14 runs while the home side only took 7 overs to win the match, losing just one wicket in the process. Meinciau reached the final of the Carmarthenshire Cup in that year but lost the match.

On July 18th 1975 I brought the Porthcawl Cavaliers down to play Meinciau. I lived in Porthcawl at the time but we were put in our place by our hosts. Meinciau scored 107 and we only managed 77 for 7 in the 20 over match. Nevertheless, we thoroughly enjoyed the Black Horse hospitality afterwards.

In 1977 Will Morgan scored a total of 477 runs in 25 innings. He was not out on two occasions which gave him an average of almost 21 runs over the season. Alan Rees and Joe Wyatt were the next two most successful batsmen. Joe Wyatt collected 56 wickets that season and Alan Rees claimed 48 victims. But it was Malcolm Evans who was the most economical bowler over the course of the season.

From 1980 the cricket team became under the umbrella of the Meinciau Sports and Recreation Committee. I believe that this was an excellent idea and the way for small communities to structure the activities within their community.

The cricket sub committee consisted of: S. Rees, M. Sadler, L. Morris, G. Samuel, R. Evans.

Meinciau played again in the Carmarthenshire Cup in 1981. On June 21st 1983 they played Glamorgan to celebrate the fiftieth anniversary of the club. In a meeting on April 11th it was decided to purchase a new kit worth £250 and to build a shed with scoreboard and purchase a new mower. It is always important to look good! In that meeting it was decided to lower the fee for the unemployed from £3.00 to £1.00.

The details of the historic game are as follows:

GLAMORGAN

	How Out	Bowler	Total
Charles Rowe	(C) Phil Gower	Steve Evans	92
Arthur Francis	(C) Alan Rees	Ken Hopkins	123
Alan Lewis Jones	(C) Phil Gower	Steve Evans	10
Mike Selvey	(B)	Ken Hopkins	32
Phil Holding	Not Out		37
Barry Lloyd	Not Out		16
John Hopkins			
Rodney Ontong			
Eifion Jones			
Malcolm Nash			
Alan Wilkins			
Lloyd		Extras	7
		Total	317

Bowler: Andrew Jones 0 for 55; Lyn Lewis 0 for 70; Alan Rees 0 for 59; Steve Evans 2 for 69; Ken Hopkins 2 for 57

MEINCIAU

Ken Hopkins	(B)	Charles Rowe	6
Peter Jones	Run Out		9
Ralph Evans	(B)	Alan Wilkins	7
Alan Rees	(St) Eifion Jones	John Hopkins	76
Andrew Jones	(B)	Charles Rowe	20

106

Garry Samuel	(St) Eifion Jones	Arthur Francis	7
Michael Evans	Not Out		11
Maelog Morris	(B)	John Hopkins	0
Phillip Gower	(C) Charles Rowe	John Hopkins	7
Geraint Rosser	(C) Malcolm Nash	Arthur Francis	6
Lyn Lewis	(C & B)	Arthur Francis	0
Steve Evans	(C) Barry Lloyd	Mike Selvey	15

Extras 4

Total 168

Bowler: Wilkins 1 for 14; Nash 0 for 28; Rowe 2 for 28; Lloyd 0 for 11; A. L. Jones 0 for 34; Francis 3 for 22; Hopkins 3 for 27 Selvey 1 for 1

It was a praiseworthy performance by the Meinciau lads in a game that they will never forget.

Although a member of the Carmarthenshire League, Meinciau also played against teams such as Carew and Neyland in Pembrokeshire and Ffostrasol and Llanilar in Ceredigion.

A match against Rosemarket in the Whitbread cup competition hit the pages of the London newspapers in 1983.

HOWZAT!

WHEN rain stopped play-between West Wales village cricket teams Rosemarket and Meinciau in the Whit-breads Championship, they agreed to settle it in the pub—at pool and darts.

After Meinciau won, 16-12, Whitbreads said they didn't approve officially, but it seemed a gentlemanly way to settle it.

A match that stands out was an away match against the Mond Nickel team in the Swansea Valley on the 31st of July 1983. The home team batted first and scored 273 for 5 wickets. In reply, Meinciau scored 241 with Phil Gower 75 and Peter R. Jones 61 making valiant efforts on behalf of the visitors who put up a great fight in quite a wonderful match. In complete contrast on the 24th of May 1984 Five Roads could only manage 10 runs in eleven overs in a match at Meinciau. There were six ducks in their innings and A. Jones tore through their batting, taking 7 wickets for 3 runs. Meinciau only took 3 overs to win the match allowing the boys plenty of time to refresh themselves in the bar afterwards.

On occasions, neighbouring cows would have a change of scenery, according to the minutes of November 12th 1984 and would fancy a game on the hallowed ground. Derek Rowlands was delegated the task of being the spoil sport by blocking off the escape route the cows had created in the hedge.

Meinciau pulled out of the league in 1985 due to the state of the field but a year later the team rejoined. An important decision was taken when it was decided to form an under 13 side in a meeting held on the 12th of January 1987. This would ensure a steady stream of youngsters filtering through to play for the senior team. By this time membership was £10 with a 50p subscription for every game.

With such wonderful facilities the field was in great demand and in 1991, after joining the Carmarthenshire League, Llangyndeyrn was granted permission by the committee to use the field as their home base on the understanding that they paid £20 a month and helped to maintain the wicket.

On May 22nd 1993 Meinciau won the Stepney Bowl. From 1994 onwards Mynyddygarreg also used the field for their home games. By that time both clubs were playing in the Village League which resulted in keenly contested local derbies. The Carmarthenshire League was facing difficulties and it soon disbanded because clubs were facing problems in fielding teams on weekends since the games were over 40 overs and therefore taking up a considerable chunk of the day. The 20 over Village League could be played during weekday evenings and seemed more attractive and certainly more convenient to many.

Craig Howells was the main batsman in 2001 with an average of 36 runs for the season. Aled Williams and Paul Rees with averages of 22 and 15 respectively were useful performers. Craig Rees, Paul Rees, Rene Smith, and Andrew Harding were the most successful bowlers with a collection of 14, 13, 9 and 8 wickets respectively.

The Village League produced an excellent competition but, unfortunately, due to the state of the field after a series of poor summers Meinciau had to withdraw from the League in 2008. But before the withdrawal from the League Meinciau won the Plate competition and followed that by winning the cup on the 7th of August 2005. Llanwrda was the opposition but the Meinciau opening batsmen were in brilliant form with Craig Howells scoring an unbeaten 156 and the excellent Joe Wyatt still there at the end of the innings with a steady 48 to his name. In reply, Llanwrda were bowled out for 161 with Aled Williams grabbing 2 wickets, Craig Howells 2, Mark Hewitt 2 and Nathan Lewis 1 being the successful bowlers. To complete Llanwrda's misery there were 3 run outs as well. The following season Meinciau retained the cup beating their near neighbours Mynyddygarreg (winners of the plate in 2005) in the final. Craig Howells 28 and Mark Hewitt 15 were the main batsmen in a score of 80 for the cup holders. Mynyddygarreg were bowled out for a total of 71 with Andrew Harding, Kieren Evans and Aled Williams being the main wicket takers.

The captain over the last ten years has been Paul Rees who is a fine example of someone coming through from the junior ranks and who has benefited from the structure within the club. Paul, together with his father Alan, has given wonderful service to the club. Let's hope that there will be a cricket team in the village again before long. Several generations of locals have gained a great deal by having had the opportunity of playing cricket for Meinciau – a club that has an interesting history, a history that deserves a future as well.

ROBERT MORGAN

Robert Morgan was a Bancffosfelen boy but due to the fact that his mother Margaret was a Meinciau girl his mother's village has a claim on him as well! Margaret was the daughter of Henry and Harriet Morris, 'Meinciau Mawr'. She married Wyn Morgan and David Robert Ruskin Morgan was born on August 29th 1941. Tragically, Margaret died following the birth of Robert's sister, Siân.

He was educated at Ysgol Bancffosfelen and Ysgol Ramadeg y Gwendraeth, where he soon showed his potential as a rugby player. Ray Williams, the Llanelli and Wales winger, was the P.E. teacher in the school and he advised the club that they should have a good look at a certain Robert Morgan. On this recommendation the Gwendraeth Valley schoolboy was selected to play for Llanelli against Cardiff in a mid week fixture at Stradey Park. The player in direct opposition to Robert was the experienced Welsh international Gordon Wells who had been capped seven times by his country. The young schoolboy had a brilliant game and gave his illustrious opponent a torrid time. Robert Morgan quickly made the right wing berth his very own. Playing inside him in the centre was Ken Jones who was also a product of Ysgol Ramadeg y Gwendraeth. In contrast to Robert, Ken was a member of the highly successful Welsh Secondary Schools team and was good enough, according to the press, to play for Wales while still at school. Robert Morgan never played for Wales as a schoolboy and consequently escaped the adulation of the press which resulted in him not being subjected to that sort of pressure. This may well have been to his advantage.

He soon became a huge favourite at Stradey and every time he received the ball one could feel the buzz reverberating through the crowd. His speed together with his electrifying outside swerve left his would be tacklers floundering. The Welsh selectors were highly impressed and on January 20th 1962 Robert Morgan gained his first cap for Wales playing on the right wing in a 0-0 draw against England at Twickenham. The Welsh team that day was as follows:

Kel Coslett; Robert Morgan; Dewi Bebb; Ken Jones; Malcolm Price; Alan Rees; Lloyd Williams (Captain); Len Cunningham; Bryn Meredith; Kingsley Jones; Brian Price; Roddie Evans; Robin Davies; Haydn Morgan; Alun Pask.

While he was at Stradey Robert played nine times for Wales. He then moved on to Cardiff but he never played for his country again. He became injury prone and eventually retired from the game.

He trained as a teacher at Cardiff Training College but after a short stint as a P.E. teacher he spent the majority of his career in the oil industry. He lived in the Gower with his wife Jen and son Rhydian and was at one time the captain of Pennard Golf Club. Sadly, after a game of golf on September 19th 1999, Robert died suddenly at the relatively young age of 58.

The Black Horse Connection

I believe that a vibrant society requires good strong roots. Even a mobile society that is so characteristic of modern life needs to identify itself with the past. The history of the Black Horse embraces the lives of many people who have strong connections with Meinciau. My own family is tied closely to the Black since my mother, my grandmother and great grandmother were all born there.

The Black Horse has always played a central role in the life of the village. It has, in the course of time, also doubled up as a slaughter house and as the home of Meinciau Rovers AFC.

For many years it has been a free house and it has attracted customers from far and wide especially when Llanelli played their home matches on a regular basis every other Saturday at Stradey Park and before matches were geared to the demands of the television timetable. In my humble opinion television has been the curse of Welsh rugby with the timing of matches arranged without any consideration for the supporters.

The landlady at the time was Nance Williams, my grandmother's sister, and she would prepare plates of sandwiches ready for the hungry and, of course, thirsty customers on their return journey from Stradey. Nance was a legend in her own lifetime – everyone knew Nance and what was more important Nance knew everyone as well. She kept a well run pub – there was never any trouble in the Black. There were a few lock-ins occasionally and whether the police knew of this I don't know but the police themselves organised a few parties there from time to time.

There was one occasion when the London Welsh Male Voice Choir called in the Black on their way home from the 1974 National Eisteddfod held in Carmarthen. The celebrations went on long after the last pint should have been drawn. This time, however, an officious policeman called to see what was going on but Nance soon enlightened him by stating that the London Welsh Choir were celebrating because they had won the Grand National!

Over the years the Black proved to be one of the most popular pubs in the area. It was the local for many who lived well outside the village. The walls of the Black could tell many a tale and witnessed nights that gave great joy to so many people. The singing generated every Saturday night would do any choir proud.

The history of the Black goes back a long time. It was once a part of the Stepney Estate. There is reference to the Black in the Surveys of the Stepney Estate 1724-1840 while in the Stepney Rent Book of 1909 there is the following information:

Rent per year – £16. Public House on main road from Llanelli to Carmarthen. Licensed 4 rooms downstairs 4 rooms upstairs. Stable with 5 stalls. Building very old and in bad repair. Roof leaks and will require renewal. 3 casks (185 gallons) per week. That is a lot of drinking! *The land is used for accommodation purpose and is in excellent state of cultivation. The tenant is a butcher thus a slaughterhouse is attached to the public house. £16 a year appears an exceptional low rent for these premises and fields.*

On July 19th 1851, at Llangyndeyrn Parish Church, John Williams, son of John and Sarah Williams of the Black Horse, married Mary Benbough of Gellygatrog. Mary was the daughter of Edward and Elizabeth Benbough. Edward, my great, great, great grandfather was born in Eardisley Here-fordshire in 1780. He was the son of Henry and Elizabeth (née Williams) Bengough. Apparently, it was Edward who changed the Bengough (that can be traced to the Welsh Ben Goch) to Benbough. Why he changed his surname is a mystery but the Benbough clan has, since then, become quite numerous in the locality. Edward married Elizabeth Hughes, who was 18 years younger than him, on the 19th of May 1818 in Llanafan Church in Cardiganshire. Edward was a customs and excise officer and the family lived in Aberporth, Llandysilio and Lower Solva before moving to the Meinciau area.

One of his seven children, Isaac, emigrated in 1888 to California with his family and started an undertaker's business. One of Isaac's children, James Percival Benbough, became an influential and a distinguished Republican politician in California. His first job was running a grocery as well as a men's clothing store. After his father's death he expanded his

112

father's undertaker business. James Percival was elected to the San Diego council and served between 1913-1917 when he was also superintendent of the fire department. In 1931 he was appointed police chief, and he endeavored to break up cliques and fight the corruption which existed in the police department. However, after only three months in office he resigned due to frustration in removing entrenched corruption. He was elected mayor of San Diego in 1935 and re-elected in 1939. Part of his accomplishments as mayor was to help prepare the city for World War II. He died in office on November 4th 1942 – the only San Diego mayor to die in office. James Percival Benbough and his wife Grace Legler Benbough had two sons. Their son, Percy J. Junior, was killed in a plane crash on February 20th 1932 at the age of 25. Their other son, George Legler Benbough, took over the family's undertaker business in the 1930s. The business was expanded after his father's death to become the largest group of undertakers in the USA and during his life time George Legler Benbough gave over one million dollars to the San Diego Musuem of Art. He died aged 89 in 1998 and since he had no direct heirs, with the huge fortune he had amassed from his business he established the Legler

James Percival Benbough on the right with President Roosevelt and the Governor of California.

Benbough Foundation which promotes improvement in the quality of life for the citizens of San Diego.

But from San Diego let us come back to Meinciau and to the Black Horse. Edward and Elizabeth Benbough's daughter Mary, sister of the Californian exile Isaac, and her husband John Williams made their home in the Black Horse. Mary's parents showed considerable opposition to her relationship with John. This has a familiar ring to it as it has been a common occurrence throughout the ages. The famous Welsh play, *Y Ferch o Gefn Ydfa*, depicts this situation very well but Mary ignored parental opposition and married John. By the time of the 1861 Census the marriage had produced three children; Edward, David and Richard. Also living in The Black was John's brother David who was 28 years of age. There is evidence that there was another child as well by the name of Isaac, probably named after his uncle.

John Williams died and Mary was remarried in Pontyates church to John Morris, Mansant Fach, on March 25th 1864. John and his family came to Mansant Fach from Glan Hiraeth, Mynyddygarreg. John was a butcher and it was when he moved in with his new wife that the slaughterhouse became part of The Black Horse and remained so for many years. John was very fond of his drink and he also enjoyed singing. He was a well known figure in the various local establishments, especially The Lamb and Flag and The Prince of Wales in Mynyddygarreg. He would enjoy his few beers and then he would render his party pieces, "Bachgen Main" and "Blodyn Du." This marriage produced five children – John and Elizabeth, both born in 1865, Joseph and Henry born in 1868 and Priscilla who was born in 1874. Unfortunately, Priscilla died at the tender age of six. The following verse appears on her gravestone:

Weep not for me my parents dear
I am not dead but sleeping here
If life was short I have longer rest
God called me when He thought best.

The 1901 census indicated that Mary and John lived in The Black Horse with their son, also called John, granddaughter Priscilla, who was 13 at the time and two servants Sarah Morris and James Williams. Unfortunately, John, Mary's husband, died on the 19th of September 1905 following an accident on the Trimsaran mountain road to Pembrey. He was visiting Tynewydd Farm, and having had a few beers on the way, he fell from his trap and dislocated his spine. It was his son John who took over as licensee as referred to in the 1909 Stepney Rental Book.

Their daughter Elizabeth, my great grandmother, married William Jones, a coalminer, and they had nine children. Priscilla, Joseph, Mary Ann, Elizabeth, Maurice, Stephen, Edward, Alice and Nance. Priscilla was named after her mother's sister. She married John Bowen of Tanybanc at Bethel Chapel, Llangyndeyrn, on the 26th March 1918. But why marry in Llangyndeyrn when both were Meinciau people and Priscilla was one of the organists in Moreia? Apparently William, her father, was thrown out of the chapel due to the fact that he kept a public house, even though The Black Horse family had always been staunch chapel members. Possibly Priscilla was so devastated by this narrow minded act that she decided to marry in Bethel. They went to live in Hafod y Gân, a new house built by her husband John for £909-3-8 Their marriage however was cut tragically short since Priscilla died on the 30th of June 1923 of Valvular disease of the heart. They had one child, Eirwen, who was my mother.

Elizabeth remained in The Black Horse until her death in 1945, nine years after she lost her husband William. By that time her daughter Nance had taken over the pub together with her husband Thomas John Williams who became one of the great characters of the village. It was an enormous loss to the family and to the village as a whole when Thomas John died in 1960.They had one child, Marie who married Malcolm Evans from Carway. Malcolm was an assistant mining engineer and a keen cricketer who possessed a dry sense of humour. Following his death on March 4th 2005 Marie has kept The Black Horse open, although, nowadays, only on three nights of the week. In fact, The Black Horse has remained in the same family for over 160 years.

One of Elizabeth's brothers was Henry Morris who was born in 1871. Henry, like his father, was a butcher and he married Harriet Evans who lived in Caegwyllt, a farm on the Meinciau to Bancffosfelen road. Harriet conceived on twenty-three occasions, losing seven due to miscarriages. The list of children with their dates of birth, place of birth and date of death makes interesting reading:

	Date of birth	Place of birth	Date of death
Wil	1890	Caegwyllt	1968
Mary Ann (Nancy)	1891	Meinciau Bach	1976
John	1893	Meinciau Bach	1959
Margaret (Maggie)	1895	Tŷ Canol	February 1907
Charlotte (Lottie)	1896	Tŷ Canol	1973
Richard	1897	Tŷ Canol	1978
Bridget Tugela	1900	Tŷ Canol	1969
Jennie Priscilla	1901	Tŷ Canol	February 1907
Rhodie Selina	1902	Tŷ Canol	1988
Donna Camille	1903	Tŷ Canol	1904
Sage	1904	Green Hill	February 1907
Poppy Magdalene	1906	Green Hill	May 1907
Luther Daniel	1907	Green Hill	1909
Colwyn Benbough	1908	Green Hill	1966
Olive Doreen (Pinc)	1909	Green Hill	2001
Margaret Valerie	1916	Meinciau Mawr	1949

It is remarkable to think that nine members of this large family at one time lived in Tŷ Canol which was only a two room cottage.

Three children died from diphtheria within a week of each other in February 1907. Sage on the 2nd; Margaret (Maggie) on the 7th and Jennie two days later on the 9th of the month. On the 29th of May 1907 their sister Poppy Magdalene also died, from Congenital Debility and Acute Bronchitis. Losing four children in the same year must have been a harrowing and devastating experience for the family.

They left Tŷ Canol to live in Green Hill before moving to Meinciau Mawr in 1912; the Morris family has remained there ever since. Henry himself died on October 14th 1919 when he was only 48 years of age. Harriet went on to live until she was 80 years old. She died on February 15th 1951 at the home of her daughter Rhodie in Carmarthen.

It was their son John, with his wife Jennie, who continued farming Meinciau Mawr. This marriage produced ten children: Jack, Maureen, Mair, Muriel, Garwyn, Cliff, Lyn, Ieuan, Gideon and Ken. Jack married Frances Gravell of Cydweli, sister of the legendary Tom who founded the well known Gravells Garage that is by now one of the most flourishing businesses in Wales. The Gravell dynasty continues in the hands of Tom's son David and grandsons Ian and Jonathan. Jack Morris, like his brothers Garwyn, Cliff and Gideon were all butchers while Gideon, in addition, remained at home to farm Meinciau Mawr. His son Maelog lives there today.

Ieuan was an enthusiastic point to point jockey and the horse My Bluff, although owned officially by his brother-in-law Cyril Morris and his wife Muriel, was much loved by the whole family. My Bluff became a well-known racehorse and was trained by John in Meinciau Mawr.

Lottie, Henry and Harriet's daughter and my grandmother, married William Thomas, son of John and Elizabeth Thomas who farmed the Ffrwd, Pontantwn. (The sharp ones amongst you will have noticed that both my grandmothers were first cousins and my great great grandmother on my mother's side and my great great grandmother on my father's side was the same woman – Mary Benbough.)

John and Elizabeth hailed from Aberlash, Llandybie. Apparently, Elizabeth was not acceptable to John's family when they were courting and consequently they went their separate ways. We are lucky in Wales that we do not have arranged marriages – I'm sure it's been quite close a few times! Anyway, Elizabeth married a local butcher and the marriage produced four children. One of the children was Lydia, who married John Thomas, Coedwalter, Llangyndeyrn. That marriage produced four children – Jennie, Lizzie Ann (the mother of Vicar Hugh Thomas), Tom and Maggie, who married David Richards, Ystradferthyr. David Richards was the secretary of Moreia Meinciau for a number of years.

Meanwhile, the despondent John went to live and work in the coal-mines of Ohio before moving out west to California. During his travels he met Billy the Kid but I doubt whether they sent Christmas cards to each other! Elizabeth's husband died and when he heard the news John came home and in due course the romance between the two was rekindled .They married on March 29th 1879. John was almost 42 years old at the time and Elizabeth ten years younger. They had six children and William, my grandfather, was one of them. John, a chapel organist, was highly thought of in his community and before he and his family moved to the Ffrwd, Pontantwn, Watcyn Wyn, the famous Welsh poet, composed verses for his friend to commemorate his departure. (See the Welsh section.)

William and Lottie began their married life in the Ffrwd before moving on to Penybanc Farm, Waun y Fran on the road from Llangyndeyrn to Llanddarog and eventually settling in Gellygatrog in 1933. This last move meant that the family was farming Gellygatrog once again. Edward Benbough and Elizabeth had retired to live with their daughter Eliza in the national school in Cydweli where, according to the 1861 census, she was the schoolmistress. Lottie and William had nine children – John, known as Jack, Margaret, Nancy, Jean, Betty, Dilys, Wyn who died when he was a baby, Rhys and Huw.

Jack married Eirwen Bowen of Torcefen, daughter of John Bowen and Priscilla, who died when Eirwen was only four years old. John remarried again and his second wife, Margaret Rees, hailed from Philadelphia outside Carmarthen. Unfortunately, Margaret died tragically in the bath in Torcefen on March 23rd 1956. My parents, Jack and Eirwen, were presented in 1952 with a little girl, Margaret Joyce Priscilla, who now lives with her family in Hafod Hedd which is next door to Hafod y Gân.

My grandmother Lottie's youngest sister was Margaret who was born in 1916 – the same year as my father. Yet, Margaret was his aunt. Olive Doreen, otherwise known as Pinc, or Aunty Pinc to most of the family, was a delightful lady who spent all her working life in the health service, working for many years in Morriston Hospital before moving as matron to the hospital in Merthyr. She eventually retired to Crwbin.

My grandfather John Bowen was the son of David and Rachel Bowen. David was killed in the quarry in 1897 when he was only 31 years of age. They had four other children – Mary who died in 1886, Charlotte, who married Joshua Walters, Anne who married Henry Hall and had three children and Leticia who emigrated to Australia in 1913. Leticia, at the time, was courting William Williams, Tŷ Bach who had left for New South Wales, Australia, in 1911 where they eventually married and had three children Jack, Dave and Gwen. It must have been an extremely painful decision, leaving the family and friends behind possibly never to see them again, as was the case here. Thousands of Welsh people made this very decision in the previous century. Four thousand people from Cardiganshire settled in Ohio and there was the Patagonia adventure where the Welsh language is still spoken.

William himself was killed in a mining accident in 1938 and although he and Leticia never returned to Wales their daughter Gwen, together with her husband George, came over and stayed in Blaenlline with Gwen's cousin Elizabeth and daughter Priscilla Melville Jones, affecionately known as Baps. Since then Lynette and Pauline, George and Gwen's children, have been over several times and even Pauline's children have visited the old country by now. The world is becoming so accessible – Newcastle in New South Wales, Australia, where they live, is only twenty-four hours away. When William and Leticia emigrated it would have taken them several months to reach their destination. Pauline, recently, on the spur of the moment decided to come over for a few days to see Prince William and Kate Middleton's wedding and of course to visit some of her family around Meinciau. It is indeed a small world.

Baps herself went to work as a nurse in Australia and New Zealand between 1949 and 1953. While in Australia she worked in hospitals in Melbourne, Brisbane, and on the outskirts of Sydney. She worked in two hospitals in New Zealand, one in Wellington and the other in Taumarunui around 200 miles south west of Auckland. Baps maintains that the experience she gained in the mainly Maori hospital in Taumaunui was invaluable. When she first arrived there tuberculosis was prevalent and the Maoris believed that the hospital was a place where people went to die. But a new doctor arrived and changed the people's perceptions. A very sick person was admitted with tuberculosis. He recovered from this dreadful disease and was discharged. This had a profound effect on the local Maori population and from then on they had a far more positive attitude towards the hospital.

Nance remained in the Black all her life and her siblings also remained within close proximity to the family home. Mary was in Bancffosfelen, Stephen in Blaenlline, Joseph in Brynmoir, Priscilla in Hafod y Gân, Alice in Awelfan and Edward in Penybryn. The Black Horse, either directly or indirectly, has played a central role in the lives of many people in the past 160 years, not just locally but across the sea to far off places as well.

Siop Ley and Village People

There was no place in the world with a shop like Siop Ley. Let us go inside and see what it's like. We go through the doorway and we enter a dark passage with a wooden partition on one side. Once the passage is cleared we are in the shop. We are in the bedroom, since the bed is in front of us with the daily papers on the bed. We are in the en suite (the essential pot is under the bed). We are also in the kitchen and lounge and sitting room. Ley's shop is where she lives – a one room establishment. There is a bench alongside the bed and if one person sits at one end, with no-one else sitting on it, the other end will shoot up and the solitary figure will end up on his backside on the floor.

The shop had one small window and in front of the window was the table which was the base for Ley's cooking, eating and the counter for her transactions. The shelves that ran along the wooden partition were stacked with jars of sweets and various goods that answered the needs of the villagers.

The fireplace was to the left of the bed and Ley would feed the fire with her hands. I never once saw her use a spade or a shovel. To me as a child God had been quite generous when he made Ley and if I or other children called in the shop for some sweets when she was putting coal or "pele mond" on the fire she would go over to the appropriate jar and rummage for a large handful of boiled, paperless sweets. The washing of hands was not even considered, but we were never ill – we must have been immune to any germs.

During the 1939-45 war period rationing books came into existence. These were introduced in order to control the demand for and the cost of food. Bread and potatoes were only rationed after the end of the war; bread from 1946 to 1948 and potatoes for a short period of time from 1947. Tea, however, was rationed throughout the war until 1952, sugar and eggs until 1953, one year before the rationing books came to the end of their usefulness. It was suggested that Ley had her favourite customers and occasionally the demands of the rationing books were conveniently forgotten.

Ley was extremely generous to us as children and everyone who passed the scholarship was given three pence as a reward. She was, however, the victim of some jokes that went too far on occasions. One youngster, who shall be nameless, once filled a churn with water, leaned it against Ley's door, before knocking and running away. Ley opened the door and the inevitable happened – the water simply poured into the shop!

Ley's shop, as well as answering many of the villagers' needs, was a meeting place. The huge chain stores that have been built on the outskirts of our major towns today have become materialistic cathedrals in our society. Ley never enjoyed any great wealth but she derived great pleasure from discussing local matters and issues with her customers – young and old alike. That was Ley's wealth.

Marged y Bryn
Margaret Walters, or Marged y Bryn as she was known, was the chapel's caretaker for almost eighty years. It is said that she began her responsibilities when she was sixteen years of age and she remained as the caretaker until 1965 and when she died in 1967 she was 92 years old. But she was more than a caretaker. Marged, or Miss Walters as we the children called her, lived her life for the chapel – literally. She slept at her home in the Bryn, a small cottage about a quarter of a mile along Heol Meinciau Mawr and then she spent the whole day in the vestry where she made and ate all her meals. That was her routine, day in day out. She kept both the vestry and the chapel in an immaculate condition. We as children dare not put our feet on the benches – Miss Walters was watching us from her vantage point at the back of the vestry.

Before the days of electricity Marged was responsible for lighting the chapel – not an easy task in those days. There was a building outside the chapel that housed a trough where Marged mixed carbide with water to generate the gas that was piped through to the chapel. Inside the chapel were a number of lamps that were lit by Marged before the service. The arrival of electricity in the village was quite a change for her.

In 1963 Marged received the Gee Medal in recognition of her services to the chapel. As far as I am aware Marged did not miss one single service until her health deteriorated at the very end of her life. What a wonderful record!

Apparently, Marged was quite fond of her brandy and unknown to everyone, including the deacons she used to have her daily fix from Nance the Black, which was very convenient since the Black was next door to the vestry.

She was at one time engaged to John, who was the son of John and Mary Morris the Black and Nance's uncle, but nothing developed from the courtship and both remained unmarried.

Will Brynbarre

Will Brynbarre, or Will Sage as he was known locally, was quite a character. His proper name was Will Evans and he was married to Sage – hence Will Sage. Will and Sage had two children – Mair and Glenys. Mair died when she was only 28 years old. Glenys married Danny Phillips, 'Drynllwyn', Four Roads, and they in turn had two children Delme and Lon.

Will and Sage lived in 'Morning Star', opposite the Black Horse and Will found that set up to be more than handy. He was a miner who usually worked the night shift and he would go to the mart in Carmarthen without bothering to sleep. Will went to the mart one Wednesday, as was his usual practice, but on this occasion he came back early and decided to call in the Black before returning home. Sage was oblivious to this but Will's dog wasn't. He knew where his master was and he decided to cross the road, lie down on the door step and wait for Will. When coming back from the toilet Will noticed that his dog was on duty outside the front door. He knew that this would have informed Sage of the whereabouts of her husband. He gave his dog a kick up his backside and shouted (in Welsh) "Cer gartre y clapgi diawl" – "Go home you bloody gossiper."

Morning Star was a smallholding and Will was in his element amongst his pigs, cows and calves. He did not drive, so every Wednesday he travelled to the mart in Carmarthen by bus or by pony and cart. When he travelled by bus and if he bought a piglet, he would bring it home on the bus, usually in the upstairs department, while any calf that was bought would have to be satisfied with a ride on the lower deck of the bus. Whether South Wales Transport charged for the transport of the occasional calf or pig, I do not know. What chance would there be of that happening today?

Since he kept pigs Will had an arrangement with Ysgol Gwynfryn regarding the swill. This was collected every day from the school and the Meinciau children in the top class had the responsibility at the end of each day of carrying the bin, which was full to the rim, on to the bus. The bin was placed on the platform but by the time the bus reached Meinciau the platform was flooded with remnants of the school dinners. The bins were then taken to Morning Star and Sage invariably rewarded us with tomato sandwiches. Will died aged 67 in 1961 while Sage was 81 when she died in 1969.

Dewi Gravell

Dewi was the latest person from Moreia to study for the ministry. He was a pupil of Ysgol Gwynfryn and then Pontyberem Secondary Modern before leaving school at the age of fifteen. He obtained work in a men's clothing shop in Carmarthen.

Dewi possessed a lovely but mischievous personality. He was very popular with everyone and as a youngster sitting in the back corner seat in Moreia life was always interesting, even if the sermon was dire, for Dewi would always be up to something. Ann Pen Tyle's hat would often take off as she sat down at the end of a rousing hymn and inevitably Dewi would be responsible! Fits of laughter would often emanate from that particular corner of the chapel, while Dewi, wearing the innocent look, would often be the main instigator. He was great company during the various outings that the Young People's Society embarked on.

However, in his early twenties Dewi decided to go in for the ministry and he gave up his job to study in Bala Bangor Theological College. But during the summer holidays in 1970 he went, one day, to join his brother who was on holiday in Tenby. Tragically, Dewi drowned while swimming in the sea. The whole community was in deep shock and mourned the loss of such a wonderful, gregarious and capable person.

Dai Rees

Although I never met Dai Rees I still feel that I know him because I have heard so much about this somewhat eccentric person. He lived with his wife Kate in 'Tŷ Canol' which was one of the whitewashed cottages. Dai was a keen gardener and every year there was a competition amongst the villagers as to whose garden would yield the first early potatoes. Dai would inevitably be the first every year. Dai was the first to own a car in the village and it was a mystery how he could afford to buy a car, having had to give up his job as a miner due to ill health. It was not any sort of car – it was similar to the ones shown in various films and the one Al Capone used to drive. Dai thought so much of the car that it was covered with a shroud and kept in a garage in a field that since became known as 'Cae Garage'.

The car was not used very often but when it was used it became quite a social event. Both Dai and Kate would be dressed in their Sunday best and Kate, wearing her large hat, would sit in the back seat and wave to the villagers as they would line the street to witness the Meinciau royals glide past them in their gleaming car.

The village children were apparently afraid of Dai. He would stand in the doorway with one hand leaning against the door frame with the other grabbing hold of his belt that circled his enormous girth. From afar the children felt safe and they often provoked Dai by chanting out:

> *Dai Rees cawl pys*
> *Dala chwannen*
> *Ar ei grys*
> *Bob nos fel y cloc*
> *Dala chwannen*
> *Ar ei .....!*

The Awelfan Boys:

Maurice Williams

Maurice was someone unforgettable by everybody who met him. He was a larger than life personality with a body, although not athletic, to match. He was born a bonny 13lb baby on March 6th 1919 to Alice and John Williams. Alice was one of the Black Horse girls and John was a tailor who carried out his trade in a workshop in the garden of the pub. Maurice was the eldest of three brothers and he was followed by Ken who has lived in Liverpool for well over fifty years and Kerri who lives with his family in 'Awelfan', the old family home.

The only school Maurice attended was Gwynfryn and in time he joined the Royal Air Force. His father was anxious for him to join the police force but although he was tall Maurice's chest fell short of the required standard which is very difficult for anyone who knew him later on in life to believe. He bought chest expanders, but to no avail – the inches did not increase and consequently Maurice never joined the police force.

Following the end of the war Maurice attended night school for two years before joining the civil service in London.

Maurice remained in London for forty years and became a prominent figure in the life of the London Welsh community. He was a fine actor and received offers to turn professional in the West End. He performed regularly with Ryan Davies, Rhydderch Jones and Gwenlyn Parry in various plays

Maurice Williams.

and concerts that the London Welsh Society used to produce. It was said that Maurice's portrayal of Henry VIII was outstanding.

After retiring Maurice came back to live in 'Awelfan' in his home village and immediately he immersed himself in the life of the community. He used his vast experience to direct plays with the Cydweli Castle Players which were all performed in Neuadd Mynyddygarreg. One of these was 'Night Must Fall' by Emlyn Williams.

Maurice had the gift of telling a good story. One of those stories was the one about the letter he received from his mother regarding the house extension in Awelfan. Alice used to write in English:

> *Dear Maurice,*
> *The building of the extension is coming on fine. Will* (the builder and Alma Carter's father) *and I have now reached the intercourse stage.*

She meant damp course!

Maurice was not the most practical of people. He was painting the roof of his mother's shed on one occasion when he realised that he had painted around himself and he was stuck in the middle.

He did a great deal of work on behalf of the Blind in Carmarthen, working closely with Rhian Evans. He was also a prominent figure in the concert party formed by local people who performed in concerts or poems and pints evenings at venues reaching from Llanybydder to Porthcawl.

Maurice and I had the privilege of entertaining the people of Four Roads in the Salem Vestry one evening in the spring of 1986 and Maurice was in his element. However, that was the last time I saw him. He had a cold that would not clear and he was complaining of this cold every time we spoke on the telephone. Eventually, he was taken to hospital where they diagnosed strangulated hernia. This in turn led to septicaemia and Maurice passed away on May 9th 1986, 67 years of age.

Ken Williams
Ken was born on December 8th 1924. During the miners strike in 1929 the Vestry was used as a soup kitchen and one of Ken's earliest memories is being refused soup by someone in the vestry because he was not a miner's son, ignoring the fact that both his grandfathers and four uncles had been miners. There was a chalet built in 'Awelfan's' garden to cater for the Black Horse girls who had developed tuberculosis. There was no way that his grandparents could have paid for this chalet according to Ken and it was only built through the generosity of the local miners.

Following his early education in Gwynfryn, Ken went on to Carmarthen Grammar School. He was a very good rugby player and he played for the school team before going on to play for Carmarthen Quins and Pontyberem. His postion was wing forward and he scored the winning try when Pontyberem beat Tumble in front of 3,000 spectators at Tumble. It was the first time that Tumble had ever lost at home to Pontyberem.

Ken was very prominent in the activities of Moreia especially with the young people that met every Thursday in the vestry. They would prepare to perform concerts that would tour various chapels in the district. Kerri and Maurice, Megan Morris on the piano, Lyn Morris, Sal Davies Tŷ Top, Beti King, Beti Jones Blaenlline, Reg Morris and Don Jones Tŷ Cornel were the leading lights in these concerts. Ken enjoyed writing verses for these evenings and the concerts would always end with a song including these words:

Nôl at Ley, May a Magi
Sydd a'u gwên fel heulwen haf,
Nôl i'r bwthyn bach lle'm ganwyd
Rhaid i ni ddweud Nos da
Nos da.

The chapel played a central role in Ken's life and this still remains the same now in Liverpool. The chapel was thriving in the 1930s according to Ken with well over a hundred attending Sunday School which ran a Penny Bank project. Two members of the Young People Society were chosen every year to be responsible for the Penny Bank. Money would be collected every Sunday and banked. The chapel would collect the interest at the end of the year and the money would then be handed over to the contributors. This system prevailed during my time in Sunday School as well.

The Sunday School trip in August was the highlight of the year for Ken. One year it would be westwards to Tenby, Saundersfoot or Llansteffan and the following year eastwards to Aberavon, Porthcawl or Mumbles. This was the highlight of the whole year for the children although occasionally a local farmer would take them and a few parents in the horse-driven cart to Ferryside.

Like his brother Maurice, Ken joined the Air Force. He was hoping to become a pilot but unfortunately that was out of the question because Ken was colour blind and consequently he joined the Navy. After leaving the Navy, Ken studied at Liverpool University and then accepted a post with the Health Service in Liverpool where he still lives with his wife Audrey.

Ken remembers five shops in the village selling various things and this when times were difficult and poverty could be seen all around. There were men out of work and there were tramps travelling from one workhouse to the next often sleeping in the hedgerows. According to Ken one had to give them a wide berth because they hated being disturbed. They would often call in various houses usually looking for something to eat.

Ken used to play tennis with the other children on the main road. Unlike today there was hardly any traffic. Hay or straw would be the net and there were no rackets to be seen. The children's hands would suffice as rackets and this undoubtedly helped to develop good hand-eye coordination. Fred Perry, Bunny Austin and Dorothy Round were the tennis heroes of the time and they would grace the Meinciau Wimbledon every year!

He also enjoyed playing "Cat and Dog." The cat was a six-inch twig cut approximately two inches thick with both ends sharpened. A stick would then be used to hit one end and as the "cat" rose the aim was to hit it again with the stick (dog) and to measure the distance that it would travel. The boys also liked to play Spoke and Washer. The washer was a circular metal ring at least eighteen inches in diameter and two inches wide. The spoke, often made from the handle of an old bucket and straightened, acted as a brake to keep the washer or wheel, as it was sometimes called, under control. Ken and his friends used to play this game on their way back and fore to school. He also remembers playing nine steps and jump a game that involved using a stick to smash an egg that had been placed nine steps away from the child who was blindfolded. The task was for the child to find and smash the egg. Not many people succeeded. Ken recalls the cricket team playing in the 1930s. Most of the team was made up of farmers and miners with some of the miners coming straight from their shift on to the cricket field. Quoits was another popular game played in the village.

Even though Ken has by now lived in Liverpool for over sixty years Meinciau still remains a part of him. You can take Ken from the village but you cannot take the village from Ken.

Kerri Williams

Kerri was the youngest of the 'Awelfan' children. Kerri was born on 27th of December 1927 and was named Kurry in recognition of the fact that his uncle William Williams, 'Tŷ Bach', had moved to Kurry Kurry near Newcastle in New South Wales, Australia. Kerri however decided to change the U to an E and so Kurri became Kerri. He lived together with his wife Joyce and their daughter Gill in 'Hafod y Gân' as well as 6 Bryn Moreia before moving back to the old home of 'Awelfan'. One of Kerri's earliest memories is carrying water from the village pump back to the house. That was the normal practice for every household in the village at that time.

Gwynfryn was Kerri's only school apart from the school of life. He remembers clearly Miss Enid Davies, one of his teachers in Gwynfryn, teaching him the sol-ffa. He must have shown considerable musical talent while in Gwynfryn because he was asked to be an adjudicator in the school Eisteddfod whilst he was still a pupil there.

Kerri left school at the age of fourteen and worked in the Nelson Garage in Carmarthen before joining the army at the age of eighteen. After leaving the army he worked in the Blaenyfan quarry. He also worked in the gun powder factory in Pembrey, then in the coalmine and finally for 26 years with Fishers in Felinfoel before retiring.

Moreia has always played a central role in his life. As a youngster he was prominent in the activities of the Young People Society and he pro-

Maurice, Kerri and Joyce enjoying an outing.

fited greatly from the experiences he gained with them. He was baptised by M. T. Rees, one of forty that particular day and there was a prayer service every evening during the week leading up to the baptism. The chapel was very important in the life of the community with a prayer service every Tuesday evening, Sisterhood, Young People Society every Thursday and a preparation service every Friday evening before Communion, which was once a month. The children's service was also held once a month although Kerri remembers one deacon arguing strongly that the children's service should be scrapped as it was a waste of a service! Thankfully, he was ignored. In 1961 Kerri was elected as a deacon and he has been the musical director in the chapel for over fifty years, following his uncle Stephen Jones, 'Blaenlline'. He enjoys singing and has a lovely tenor voice that has been utilised and appreciated by several choirs far and near.

The first task Kerri had to undertake as a deacon was to help the rest of the deacons to collect the money for the fund set up to purchase a new pipe organ. Each deacon was given a certain area to cover and, after a great deal of walking, the money was collected which allowed the organ, at a cost of £2,084.10s.0p, to be officially opened on April 4th 1963.

Kerri made a huge contribution to the Meinciau Rovers football team. He was also a member of the cricket team and is one of the faithfuls in the

129

family pub the Black Horse. Kerri is one of the everlasting icons of the village. He has played an important role in every aspect of village life. To commemorate Kerri's 80th birthday the current minister, the Reverend Emlyn Dole, wrote some verses that reflect the fact that Kerri lives his life to the full. (See Welsh section.)

Catherine Walters
Catherine by now is the oldest person in the village. At 93 years of age she is in remarkable health. Her mind and her memory are as sharp as ever and she still drives her car, although it only sees the light of day when driving to the Senior Centre in Pontiets, that has by now unfortunately closed, and the services in Moreia. The chapel continues to be a focal point in her life and she looks forward to the Sunday service.

She is the daughter of John and Get Jones, 'Gwndwn Mawr'. She married Hubert, son of Y Rhosan, Llandyfaelog, and their son, Wyn, became a vet who settled with his family in the Chippenham area in Wiltshire. After both her parents died Hubert and Catherine continued to farm 'Gwndwn Mawr' until they retired in 1969 to live in a bungalow near the Green where Catherine still lives.

She attended Bancffosfelen School and remained there until she was fourteen years old. Therefore, Catherine could be described as a Bancffosfelen girl but on Sundays she was a Meinciau girl because she mixed with her Meinciau friends in Sunday School. She vaguely remembers the Meinciau Eisteddfod when it was held in a tent and she remembers the first car that came to the village by courtesy of Dai and Kate Rees.

People were far more inventive years ago according to Catherine. She remembers making a rag mat made from old skirts, jumpers, trousers and any old clothes that had seen better days. Farming was much harder in those days compared to the present. Catherine remembers collecting lime from the kilns in the quarry, lime which was then spread over the fields. It was the age of the horse and harvesting the hay and corn was completely different to current methods and she is positive that the summers of her youth were much warmer than the summers we have now. So much for climate warming!

Sundays were holy days and only absolutely essential work such as milking the cows and feeding the animals, was done on Sundays. But as the years rolled by, Sundays became like the other days of the week and

Catherine remembers the first time they ever ventured to undertake extra work on a Sunday in 'Gwndwn Mawr'. The weather forecast was not very good and it was decided to turn over the hay so that it could be collected from the field the following day.

"Mam was not very happy about this," said Catherine, "and there she was on the field looking around to see if anyone was watching us!"

The gypsies (now recognised as travellers) who parked their caravans for months on end near Garn Ganol would help them during the harvest period but they always called back in the winter looking for some hay to feed their animals.

She befriended their children who attended the school with her. One day one of the children died and Catherine was invited into the caravan to see the body. The inside of the caravan was covered with a white shroud. There was a certain ritual when a gypsy died. She remembers the death of one gypsy woman, Mrs Burton; her two horses were put down and her caravan burnt. Catherine found them to be friendly, offering lifts to people in their carts, like Nurse Williams who would walk everywhere to see her patients including the gypsies themselves whenever the need arose.

Catherine was very happy during her formative years and that spirit has stood her in good stead all her life. She thinks, however, that life in general is more dangerous today, although she acknowledges that radio and television may be responsible for giving her this impression by highlighting crimes that she would be unaware of many years ago.

"There were no telephones and it was the telegram that brought important news to the family." Catherine or Aunty Catherine as she is known to many people is a remarkable woman who has witnessed great changes in society and not all of them for the better.

Her son Wyn was trained at Liverpool University and Ken Williams was his guide when he first arrived in the city. After graduating as a vet in 1965 Wyn's first practice was in Harlow, Essex. He then worked in Cheltenham before moving to Chippenham in 1970 where he remained until he retired. He still lives in Christian Malford with his wife Eirlys who hails from Llanddarog.

Wyn was at one time the vet to a present member of the royal family or at least to her animals. He was also responsible for Sarah Ponsonby's animals. She owned the farm where Roddy Llewellyn and Princess Margaret used to meet. Sarah Ponsonby moved eventually to France and Wyn had to accompany the party across the Channel because he had to sign the appropriate documents, otherwise all the animals would have to be quarantined. The vet from Meinciau had a weekend to remember before he returned back to his duties the following Monday.

George Williams

George and his wife Mia lived in Meinciau Mawr with their grandchild Mari Jones. Mari lived until she was 101 years of age and therefore becoming the oldest inhabitant of the village in living memory. I will be eternally sorry that I did not heed my mother's advice to talk to Mari about life in the old village over the years. No doubt other more pressing things were the centre of my attention at the time. George Williams was not just a farmer for he also transported lime from the quarry to local farms as well as stones for the roads in the locality, using his cart pulled by Prince the horse. He was quite a character who was fond of his beer and whenever George and Prince were on their travels they always called in the 'Square and Compass', Pontiets.

One Sunday morning M. T. Rees was preaching in Carway and he asked George if he could borrow Prince. So off went M.T. on the back of Prince and everything went well until on the way back, as they approached the 'Square and Compass', Prince automatically turned into the yard of the pub.

"Not today Prince bach," said the minister, hoping that nobody could see them, "You have another master now!"

But George saw the light and drinking became for him a thing of the past.

During the time that the new Moreia Chapel was being built in the early 1880s (it was opened in 1886) many services were held in the barn in Meinciau Mawr. George became the treasurer of the chapel and remained in that position for many years. He also became a prominent member of the Parish Council and was highly respected in the community.

George died in 1912 and, following his death, his widow Mia and granddaughter Mari moved a few yards down the road to Meinciau Bach. Mari and her husband William, who was one of the carpenters in the village, had two children Lizzie and Arwyn. Lizzie married John Roberts and they also had two children Joan, who provided the information about her great great grandfather, and Alun. Lizzie died in April 1962 when she was only 43 years of age. It was the family of Henry and Harriet Morris who then moved in to Meinciau Mawr.

David Lloyd of Killay Swansea won one of the literary competitions in the Meinciau Eisteddfod with verses in memory of George Williams that can be seen in the Welsh section.

Lydia Evans

To us as children Lydia Evans was Mam Tŷ Top or Mamgu Brynbarre. The *News of the World* described her as "The Pride of the Village" after they sent a reporter to interview her on her 96th birthday.

Lydia was born in Laugharne in 1857 and was the mother of ten children, one of whom was Will Brynbarre. She had twenty-six grandchildren, twenty-nine great grandchildren and two great great grandchildren. For 27 years she was a midwife and she must have brought scores of other children into the world. When asked by the reporter about modern day life and about smoking by women she said: "It's an awful thing to see but a friend of mine died recently at the age of 99 and she smoked a pipe." That remark must have been made with tongue in cheek because I saw Mam Tŷ Top herself smoking a pipe.

She began work as a domestic servant at the age of 11 and for the first year she received no pay – only her food and old clothes. She received 25 shillings for her second year's work and just before her marriage in 1883 she was earning £10 a year.

Lydia was a prolific knitter and during the war she knitted for the Forces.

She had lived in the locality for over 45 years and she followed the fortunes of Meinciau Rovers keenly, always pleased to hear when they had won. She was looked after for many years, in her one room whitewashed cottage by her granddaughter Mary Evans. Mary always arranged a party and a concert by the village children to celebrate Lydia's birthdays in her latter years.

She died just a few days before her 98th birthday.

The Mayor of Meinciau

Meurig Williams is one of those lovable characters. He moved with his parents to 'Gorwel' where they kept a petrol station and a shop for many years. But calling in 'Gorwel' meant far more than just filling up the car; it meant putting the world to right, it meant catching up with what was happening around the village. Meurig was, like several of the village characters, a fountain of information and what he did not know he would somehow find out. There was no such thing as a quick visit to 'Gorwel'.

For many years Meurig has lived with his wife Beti in The Ashes, the estate that overlooks the cricket field, but Meurig is, thank goodness, still the same. He will talk to anyone and everybody knows him. His popularity meant that he was voted the Mayor of Meinciau by the customers of the Black Horse – a position that by now remains unchallenged. Meurig's elevated status drew the attention of both the Prime Minister and the Welsh Secretary as can be seen by the following two letters.

10 Downing Street
Whitehall

23rd, January 1979

Mr Muerig Williams,
c/o The Mayor's Parlour,
The Black Horse,
Meinciau,
Kidwelly,
Dyfed.

Dear Mr Mayor

I write, on behalf of the Cabinet, to congratulate you most sincerely on your election to the high and esteemed office of Mayor of Meinciau.

As you know, the office of Mayor is steeped in history and it is to the holders of such office that Her Majesty's Government looks for support in maintaining the government of the country at the local level. I know that in placing this honour upon your shoulders the local community in your corner of South Wales is indicating its trust in you to lead the way forward to a better Britain.

It was indeed a pleasure to talk to you on the telephone on the night of your Installation and I have since had glowing reports of the occasion from the Honorable Members from the South Wales constituencies.

In due course you will receive formal communications from Her Majesty and from the Minister of State for Wales, but I do not think it out of place here to hint that Her Majesty has indicated that your name shall figure in the Birthday Honours List.

You may count on the full support of myself and my Ministers in the execution of your noble duty.

My wife, Audrey, bids me add her congratulations to mine and to wish you every success in your new office.

I am, Mr Mayor,
Yours faithfully

James Callaghan

J. CALLAGHAN
Prime Minister

Letter from the Prime Minister to the Mayor of Meinciau.

134

HOUSE OF COMMONS
LONDON, SW1

MR MEIRRYG WILLIAMS
c#o THE BLACK HORSE
MEINCIAU
KIDWELLY
DYFED   23RD JANUARY 1979

DEAR MR WILLIAMS

I AM COMMANDED BY THE SECRETARY OF STATE FOR WALES TO OFFER, ON HIS
BEHALF, THE CONGRATULATIONS OF THE SECRETARIAT ON YOUR ELECTION TO
THE HIGH OFFICE OF MAYOR OF MEINCIAU.

THE SECRETARY IS PARTICULARLY PLEASED THAT MEINCIAU NOW HAS A MAYOR
SINCE FOR SO LONG THAT AREA HAS LACKED THE DIGNITY WHICH ONLY A MAYOR
CAN BRING TO IT.   I AM SURE THAT YOU ARE AWARE OF THE RESPONSIBILITIES
ENJOINED IN YOUR HIGH OFFICE AND THAT YOU WILL CARRY THESE WITH DUE
REGARD TO THEIR IMPORTANCE IN THE GOOD GOVERNMENT OF WALES.

AS THE PRIME MINISTER MAY HAVE INDICATED TO YOU ALREADY, IT IS ARR-
ANGED THAT YOU WILL RECEIVE RECOGNITION IN THE BIRTHDAY HONOURS LIST.
I AM NOT YET AT LIBERTY TO REVEAL THE HONOUR WHICH SHALL BE BESTOWED
UPON YOU, BUT I WOULD EXPECT IT TO BE NOT LESS THAN COMPANION OF THE
BRITISH EMPIRE.

I AM, MR MAYOR,
YOUR OBEDIENT SERVANT

S P G STANICLIFFE   PA TO THE SECRETARY OF STATE FOR WALES

Letter from the Secretary of State to the Mayor of Meinciau.

It is assumed that Maurice Williams had something to do with those
letters. Meurig also received a telephone call in The Black from the Prime
Minister, congratulating him on his achievement. Needless to say, the
Prime Minister was less than 100 yards away. Maurice was at it again!

The Singing Tradition

Meinciau people are well known for their melodic singing and I am confident that the influence of both Moreia and The Black Horse has much to do with this. Locals have the choice of two choirs Côr Glannau'r Gwendraeth is a fine ladies choir under the leadership of their knowledgeable and experienced musical director Margaret Morgan. The men can join Côr Dyffryn Tywi who have the benefit of a young, vibrant and enthusiastic lady conductor in Davinia Davies (née Harries). Both choirs are in great demand and have helped to raise a great deal of money in various concerts arranged for charity.

The Meinciau Eisteddfod, held during the early part of the last century, encouraged locals to organise parties to sing in concerts and eisteddfodau in the area. Such a group was Côr Craig y Fan with Ben Richards, Felin-

Côr Craig y Fan enjoying a picnic around 1910.

136

dre, as their director. Ben's father Joseph was first cousin to the composer of Myfanwy, Joseph Parry, whose mother Elizabeth hailed from Fferm y Graig, Mynyddygarreg. Descendants of the Richards family still live in the area and several of them, such as the actor Ioan Hefin, have inherited the musical talent of the family.

John Thomas, Bryndelyn, also had a party competing in local eisteddfodau. John used to rehearse in the vestry and on occasions would tell his choir that he was going outside to listen to them sing. As they were singing he would pop off to The Black for a quick pint, come back and congratulate everyone on the wonderful sound that they created.

The Bryndelyn family were very musical and grandson Lance Roberts, who now lives in Blackpool, has sung with various professional opera companies. Terry, Lance's older brother, used to conduct the singing in Sunday School while sister Merle was a fine pianist.

Back in the 1950s there was the Dolcoed children's choir which sang in numerous concerts and competed in various eisteddfodau as well as entertaining the inhabitants of the Coombe Cheshire Home. Their conductor was Gwynfor Jones, a probation officer, who lived with his family in Dolcoed – thus the name of the choir.

A member of the choir was Peggy Davies who remembers the choir rehearsing in Dolcoed itself, and also in both Carway and Ponthenri schools. She remembers clearly singing in what was probably the 1956 National Eisteddfod in Aberdâr because, according to Peggy, they got through the preliminaries in the morning to sing on the main stage in the afternoon. Marie Evans of the Black Horse recollects a trip to the eisteddfod in Sennybridge. Gwynfor was extremely popular with the children and he gave voice training to a number of them.

The *Mercury*, Jan 6th 1955 – Ponthenri news:

The village hall was filled to its capacity last week when the Dolcoed Juvenile Choir assisted by local artists gave an admirable programme. Mr David Morris was chairman. The concert was organised by ladies of the local Civil Defence section and the proceeds will be used for new stage equipment for the hall.

Later on that year Côr Dolcoed was back again in Ponthenri for the St David's Day concert.

Stephen John Jones, Blaenlline, together with his successor and nephew Kerri Williams have given sterling service as music directors in Moreia. Before them Moreia was also fortunate in having the talents of people like Samuel Beynon, John Thomas and his father Dafydd. Moreia was always renowned for its love of singing and the annual *Gymanfa* attracted huge congregations at both Moreia and Bethesda, Ponthenri, where it was held on alternate years. The demise of the hymn singing festival, not only in this area but throughout Wales in general is a sad loss. Moreia, in recent years, has supported the popular *Plygain* in Llandyfaelog church, where different churches, chapels and societies have participated for a number of years.

Fflur Wyn.

Meinciau is very proud of the achievements of one of its children who by now is recognised way beyond her native country as a very special talent. Fflur Wyn, daughter of Eirian and Helen Wyn, was a Meinciau girl during her formative years and attended Ysgol Gwynfryn before the family moved to Brynaman. She was highly successful on the Eisteddfod circuit gaining valuable experience before graduating from the Royal Academy of Music Opera course where she studied with Beatrice Unsworth and Clara Taylor. She has won numerous first prizes, scholarships and bursaries and has starred with various opera companies here and abroad. She is by now recognised as one of our leading sopranos.

Long may the singing tradition continue.

Erling's Story

This extraordinary story links Meinciau with Oslo, Melbourne and New Orleans.

A pregnant Norwegian woman came over to Cardiff in June 1922 and whilst in the city she gave birth to twin boys in the Norwegian Church vicarage. Her name was Elizabeth Johnsen. After the twins Erling and Fredrik were born an application was made to have the babies placed in a home for infants in Cardiff. Elizabeth had to pay an allowance to keep the boys there. At three weeks old Fred became ill and was sent to a Barnardo's home in London. It was stated that Elizabeth's ex-fiancé, back in Norway, Alfred Texe was the father and both boys were given Texe as their middle name but their mother's maiden Johnsen as their surname.

At the age of 13 months Fred was reunited with his brother Erling in the home for infants back in Cardiff, having recovered from his illness.

In October 1924 Elizabeth returned to Oslo in Norway where she rekindled her relationship with Alfred Texe before marrying him in 1926. She contributed to the upkeep of the twins but she ignored all requests from the home in Cardiff to take back the boys and eventually the payments stopped. She wrote to the custodians pleading with them to allow her two boys to be made available for adoption and to make sure that they were adopted by a good family. She also announced that the father of the boys was not Alfred Texe as was previously presumed but a man named Kristen Jesnes who was a postal worker in Oslo. Consequently, Kristen was made accountable and he contributed to their upkeep until 1928 when he married. Then all payments stopped.

In 1928 the twins were moved to the Ely Cottage Homes in Cardiff but at some stage they were separated. For the next six years they were apart and became unaware of each other's existence. Then Erling became ill and was taken to hospital where he was placed in a bed next to another boy. The boy told Erling: "You look like me and I look like you." Erling and Fred were together again!

At the age of 14 both boys were sent to work on farms in Carmarthenshire. Erling found himself in Conwil Elfed where he was told: "We don't speak English here. You will have to learn Welsh." By the time he was 16 he spoke fluent Welsh and he was treated very well by the family. Fred decided eventually to join the Royal Navy and was on the minesweepers during the war. In late 1945 he bought a house and married a woman from Consett in Durham. But while he was at sea his wife sold the house and ran away with another man. Fred returned to Carmarthenshire in 1951 but at the age of 28 he committed suicide and was buried in St Anne's Church in Cwmffrwd in an unconsecrated grave.

Erling.

In the meantime, Erling, who was by now working on a farm near Cwmffrwd, had fallen in love with a girl from Meinciau. She was Jean Lewis, 'Caerarglwyddes', sister of Dona and Vernon. They married and set up home in 'Llwynteg'. As the family grew, they moved from 'Llwynteg' to 'Maesglas' and then to Bedworth in the Midlands where Erling worked for the National Coal Board.

Until he applied for his birth certificate in the late 1960s, for the purpose of emigrating to Australia on the £10 emigration scheme that prevailed at the time, Erling assumed that his surname was Johnson. It was only then that he realised that it was Johnsen (pronounced Yoonsen). However, via Bedworth, the Johnson family from Meinciau made their way to Melbourne in Australia.

Back in Norway Elizabeth, Erling's mother, and her husband Alfred Texe were presented in 1929 with their only child Else. At the age of 21 Else went to her cousin's wedding in Detroit. On the way home to Norway she met Lars Nedland Pederson, a Norwegian American who was 14 years older than her. It was a romantic journey by boat back to Norway which

140

resulted eventually in marriage and the setting up of a home in New Orleans.

In 1952 Alfred Texe died and Elizabeth spent her winters in New Orleans and her summers in Oslo. Elizabeth never mentioned anything to Else about her two half brothers although her daughter remembers seeing a photo that her mother kept of a certain building. That building turned out to be the home where her twins were kept in Cardiff. Elizabeth died in Oslo in 1982 at the age of 82.

In 1988 Else and Lars went on holiday to Norway. The day before they departed Else received a letter from a relative containing two photographs of a woman with two babies. She was astonished and shocked when she realised later on that the babies were her half brothers.

In the meantime, Erling and Jean's daughter Mandy had traced her grandmother Elizabeth to New Orleans. By that time her grandmother was dead. She also realised that the people who lived in a certain New Orleans address in 1959 were the same people who lived there in 2002, a Mr and Mrs Lars Pederson. Mandy got in touch with them and was delighted to find out that Else was her father's half sister.

In May 2002 Mandy took her father over to New Orleans to meet his new found sister. According to Mandy both Else and Erling were similar in nature and many of the people they met remarked how similar Erling was to his late mother. Erling was absolutely delighted to have found his sister and wished that he could have found her much earlier. On February 11th 2004 Erling died and in March 2009 Else passed away aged 80.

Jean still lives in Melbourne and there have been numerous visits between the Meinciau and Melbourne families. Jean's son Darren is a fine cricketer and has played for both Meinciau and Mynyddygarreg cricket clubs on his visits over here. Recently he attended a Welsh Learner's class in Melbourne and was astonished to find out that his tutor was Gwennol Tudur from Pontiets, who was married in Moreia.

In 1972 Jean went to Florida to attend her eldest daughter Julia's wedding. She met one of the bridegroom's relatives who was stationed near Meinciau during the war. He recalled visiting "The Black Horse" one evening together with some American soldier friends. The group was entertained by a party of children singing some Welsh songs. In that party was Jean herself.

What a small world!

Sale at Meinciau Mawr, 1912.
Mia Williams, second on the left in the front row, and her family are in mourning
clothes following the death of her husband George. Mari, her granddaughter,
is fourth on the left. Also included are Elizabeth Jones, The Black, in the centre
with her daughter Nance and on the extreme right Harriet Morris.

Megan Morris (on the left) with her cousin Betty Morris, Brondeg,
are the two young girls standing. But who is sitting down with
a young Joyce Morgan on her lap?

142

Top: *Siop Sâr, which was the old Post Office.*

Left: *Back row: Ken Williams, Ivor Jones and Kerri Williams. Front Row: Alice (Ken and Kerri's mother), Brinley Jones and Glenys Evans.*

My mother (first left, back row) with Annie Ynys Fach to her left, Maurice and Lizzie, Meinciau Bach, and in the front row Ivor, Priscilla (Baps), Nancy, Olwen, Megan, Nesta and Kerri enjoying a splash in the sea. Around 1930.

143

Gwynfryn teachers in the 1930s with their headteacher, Thomas Thomas.

*Gwynfryn teachers and student teachers early 1950s
with Mr George the headteacher.*

Diana Pugh Jones' class, 1985.

Dolcoed Children's Choir.

145

Children and staff of Gwynfryn School, early 1990s.

*Coronation celebrations 1953.
Jack Williams, Blaenpant,
being escorted by Lyn Morris
and Eric Beynon.*

*Villagers being supplied with water by Sam Phillips, Blaenyfan,
during the freeze of 1963.*

147

Ken Williams, his wife Audrey and daughter Barbara from Liverpool in Torcefen with my mother and myself.

The Australian connection – descendants of William and Leticia Williams.

148

Meinciau Rovers AFC, 1953.
Committee—D. Lewis (Treas.), T. J. Williams, W. D. Williams, I. Morris, E. Lewis, L. Morris (Sec.).
T. Thomas, V. Lewis, D. Bevan, M. Jones, M. Baldwin, M. Howells, G. Griffiths, R. Morris.
V. Edmunds, B. Beresford, E. Beynon (Chairman), K. Williams (Vice-Capt.), H. Bevan (Capt.), G. Miles, I. Jones.
Mascot—Brian Lewis.

Badminton team, 1984-5.
D. Clark, D. Thomas, M. Rogers, R. Lewis.
R. Thomas, H. Lewis, Dr. G. Paul, J. Owen.

149

Dai Clark fielding on the boundary.

The 1981 cup semi-final team.

Preparing for the pig roast.

Bottle stall at the village fête.

Meinciau and Four Roads pensioners, 1976.

Cross-stitch class in the Vestry.